Our Gardens
Ourselves

Our Gardens Ourselves

Reflections on an Ancient Art

Jennifer Bennett · Camden House

Illustrations by Marta Scythes

Canadian Cataloguing in Publication Data

Bennett, Jennifer
    Our gardens, ourselves : reflections on an ancient art

Includes bibliographical references and index.
ISBN 0-921820-91-7

1. Gardening.   2. Gardens.   I. Title.

SB455.3.B45 1994   635   C94-931193-6

Printed and bound in Canada by
D.W. Friesen & Sons
Altona, Manitoba

Published by Camden House Publishing
(a division of Telemedia Communications Inc.)

Camden House Publishing
7 Queen Victoria Road
Camden East, Ontario K0K 1J0

Camden House Publishing
Box 766
Buffalo, New York 14240-0766

Printed and distributed under exclusive licence from
Telemedia Communications Inc. by
Firefly Books
250 Sparks Avenue
Willowdale, Ontario
Canada M2H 2S4

Firefly Books (U.S.) Inc.
P.O. Box 1338
Ellicott Station
Buffalo, New York 14205

Design by
Linda J. Menyes

Cover photograph by
Ernie Sparks

Cover photograph: Vines and begonias courtesy Neil's Flowers, Kingston, Ontario;
shears and branches courtesy Paradiso, Kingston, Ontario.

Dedication

Publishing is a little like gardening. As Mirabel Osler writes in *A Gentle Plea for Chaos*, "Gardening is not just a putting into the earth of some frail greenery, but like a stone thrown into a pond, garden thoughts ripple outwards towards a limitless horizon." All kinds of thoughts have rippled outwards from the village of Camden East, Ontario, since the creation of its namesake, Camden House Publishing, some 15 years ago. Camden House Publishing has now moved to Toronto; in garden terms, it is both a transplanting and a change of season. As the springtime of this business comes to a close, I would like to dedicate *Our Gardens, Ourselves* to the many people who have been most important in the creation of my own books during the past dozen years. They include David Archibald, Michael G. Bowness, Eleanor Campbell Lawrence, Catherine DeLury, Patricia Denard-Hinch, Susan Dickinson, Charlotte DuChene, Frank Edwards, Jane Good, Mirelle Keeling, Christine Kulyk, Alice Lawrence, James Lawrence, Linda Menyes, Mary Patton, Tracy Read, Marta Scythes, Merilyn Simonds Mohr and Joann Webb.

Contents

On Gardens

A couple of years ago, after more than a decade of gardening, I was about to give it up. I understood that a garden is a place of joy and beauty and peace; I understood that fact from looking at pictures and paintings of gardens and from visiting other people's gardens. I knew it from what writers told me. I also knew it from my gardens of years past, which I could now enjoy in the rosy glow of recollection, and I imagined it in my gardens of the future, which would reach such perfection that I would be able to sit down and actually enjoy them. In my mind's eye, I could see them in all their glory—the paths, the perennials, the arches hung with vines, the dappled sunshine, the speckless foliage. These imaginary gardens looked remarkably like some of those pictures in books superimposed in front of my house.

But my own garden right now was a different matter. As the English poet Alexander Pope wrote, "My garden, like my life, seems to me every year to want correction and require alteration." Most people, I have found, are discontented with their gardens. Most of us are so aware of the need for corrections and alterations that we can scarcely enjoy what we have created. My own anxiety stemmed from the fear that my garden did not live up to what I thought people expected a garden writer's garden to look like. It was as simple as that. I imagined that visitors wanted Longwood or Sissinghurst. They wanted a garden centrefold, its dying foliage and thriving weeds airbrushed away. They wanted my garden to fulfill their own images of perfection, and I wanted to please them. I had all kinds of excuses for having failed them, but none satisfied me. After a while, all this feeling apologetic became irritating. I resented the garden for letting me down. When perfection did happen, it was too little, too late. Sometimes nobody was around to witness the miracle but me, and I was too busy weeding to take much notice either. Work in the garden felt like a duty being performed for a master who was never satisfied. Worse, this master kept changing the job description by throwing in bad seeds, bad weather and endless duties that took me away from the demands of the garden just when it most needed me.

I saw an old man of Corycus, who owned some few acres of waste land, a field neither rich for grazing nor favourable to the flock nor apt for the vineyard; yet he, setting thinly sown garden-stuff among the brushwood, with borders of white lilies and vervain and the seeded poppy, equalled in his content the wealth of kings.
—*Virgil, Georgics IV, 3rd century B.C.*

So when I anticipated moving to the place where I live now, I thought I just might not have a garden at all. In terms of potential, the new place was a landscaper's dream. Its shallow layer of dry soil over limestone was a challenge, but the long lawn sloping gently toward the south and west was all promise. Nevertheless, I turned to piano lessons and singing to satisfy my creative urge. I ignored what was waiting for me at my new home: a patch of Chinese lanterns, an aged and very grassy row of irises, day lilies and peonies beside the driveway and a small foundation planting beside the kitchen of juniper and yew and variegated dogwood with a lot of catnip underneath. Not much to look at, but at least it wasn't my fault.

And then, just before I moved, something happened. I started to see the garden where I still lived as though it were now in my past, and I realized how beautiful it was. As I packed and got ready to leave, it no longer made demands upon me. Now I could celebrate it in all its lovely imperfection. What an incredible thing it was, this interplay of light and air and water, earth and plants, this chorus of many parts, all in a shifting counterpoint harmony. Some of it was done by me, but a lot of it was not. One day, colour might be the dominant feature; the next day, wind; the next, rain. Freshly inspired, I found myself planting fruit trees at my new home, planning a pathway and setting up a little nursery of cuttings from my old garden. I sowed a wildflower seed mixture in a bare patch of soil and had an instant garden, including a couple of fabulous annual daisies I never could identify. Recaptured again by the magic of the garden, I realized I could not live happily without it, but I worried that my enthusiasm might evaporate as my focus narrowed again at my new home.

For as the earth bringeth forth her bud, and as the garden causeth the things that are sown in it to spring forth; so the Lord God will cause righteousness and praise to spring forth before all the nations.
—Isaiah 61:11

And so, out of my dilemma, this book was born. I needed a larger perspective. I wanted to be able to enjoy my new garden every day, not only in anticipation or memory. Other gardeners, I suspected, needed the same thing, even though they were not garden writers with an imaginary reputation to uphold. I wanted to find out about the forces that were at work besides myself—because I was certainly not the only source of energy in the garden. What was the sense in being frustrated by the wind, the clouds, the rain, the frost? And what was it they were up to anyway? All of us were working together on this effort, the garden, and I knew scarcely anything about the other influences. It was like raising children without knowing who their friends were or what they were learning at school.

I also wanted to find out why I continued to want to garden, because my original interest—the desire to raise pesticide-free food cheaply—had faded. Whatever it was that kept me gardening, I determined, was probably keeping other people gardening too. I went to a landscape-design workshop given by Julie Moir Messervy, a Boston author and landscape designer. "I believe we all have a garden within ourselves, and the ideal is to make that idea manifest," said Messervy. Most of the people who came to her workshop were landscape designers like herself, involved in the difficult game of figuring out not what they wanted—which is hard enough—but what other people wanted. Messervy pointed out that most clients were unconsciously seeking an image from their childhood, and it would help the designer if he or she could find out what that image was. The remembered scene might be in a city or the country, and it might not be a real garden but another place associated with peace, happiness and security: the seashore, a public park, a forest, a library, a summer cottage. This image, retained in some sunny corner of the memory, is forever sought in the new landscape. It is, perhaps, an unattainable ideal, the place where we knew nature before innocence was lost: our own Garden of Eden.

What are gardens? Who are gardeners?
Where does the thrust to make places of beauty,
secrecy or seclusion come from?
—*Mirabel Osler,* A Gentle Plea for Chaos, *1989*

The gardener whose elusive picture is a remembered place in a different climate will face the greatest challenge in trying to create a garden that will satisfy. Winters may simply be too harsh where we live now, summers too hot and dry or horticultural fashions too strange. Still, the perseverence of gardeners is manifested by the fascinating diversity of gardens that appear now in cosmopolitan cities: the spare Japanese garden; the southern European garden with its overhead grape vines; the Chinese garden with its raised beds of green vegetables; the English garden of tea roses and staked delphiniums. Maintaining these gardens may be an ongoing struggle against the climate and the expectations of the neighbours.

One famous such transplant was Napoleon's wife Josephine, a native of Martinique who became a devoted, even obsessive gardener in France and who is best remembered for the mid-18th century's largest collection of roses. Their fragrances and colours brought the lushness of her remembered tropics to the greenhouses and geometrically designed beds of her adopted country. To France, Josephine introduced eucalyptus, hibiscus, dahlias and rare tulips, and her maiden name, la Pagerie, was given to a tropical vine, the Chilean bellflower (*Lapageria rosea*). She sent for jasmine from Martinique and is reported to have said, "The seeds were sown and tended by my own hands—they remind me of my country, my childhood and the ornaments of my adolescence."

People who garden close to their childhood home find it easier to create a satisfying garden. Gertrude Jekyll became intimately acquainted with plants as a child in England, where she gave the most beautiful ones names because she considered them her friends. So began the life's work that would make her the most outstanding woman landscape designer of her country in the 19th century.

As a child, Jekyll "used almost to worship" a certain andromeda, a pieris. Children are not inhibited by adult definitions of propriety or aesthetics, and their senses are more acute. I have a German-born friend who labours to create a spectacular garden on Ontario granite and who remembers how she and her friends would eat the pods of opium poppies—

A garden really lives only insofar as it is an expression of faith, the embodiment of a hope and a song of praise.
—*Russell Page,* The Education of a Gardener, *1962*

which were raised for their seeds and used in baking—until they all fell into a contented slumber in the sun. I remember calling the *Centaurea montana* in my family's garden "peach flower" because of its distinct fragrance, which I cannot detect at all now. More puzzling, I remember eating with my friends not only blackberries but also the petals of the wild white morning glories that clambered over the roadside hedges we passed on the way to school. They tasted bitter, but the sensation on the tongue was ethereal.

I grew up in Vancouver, on a big mountainside property from which you could see the sea. It was a place where rain sometimes fell for weeks at a stretch and vegetation was so exuberant that it had to be beaten back, not encouraged. The garden, which was terraced down the mountain slope and backed by native Douglas firs, was obviously the work of someone both devoted and expert, so encyclopaedic was its plant collection. There were many fruit trees: apples, crab apples, peaches, plums, quinces, sour cherries and a 'Bing' sweet cherry taller than the two-storey house. There were roses, hydrangeas, azaleas and flowering bulbs. Under my family's laissez-faire regime, the garden gradually became more overgrown, more mysterious, its lawns mossier and its drystone rock walls less vertical. The rose arbour rotted. Slugs lived in the shadows. The back of the property reverted to a rainforest tangle of ferns, blackberries and salal. In the farthest corner, entirely hidden from the house by a wall of towering evergreens, was a huge tree stump, relic of the virgin forest, on which the boy next door and I would sit and eat, without any feeling of remorse, the carrots we had pulled from another neighbour's garden. It was, now that I think of it, paradise.

When I came to Ontario, I had that abundant West Coast image in mind, and I was lucky enough, in my first country house, to have a property with enormous white pines and deep soil. There wasn't much of a garden when I arrived, and the two of us, the garden and I, developed together. The garden was a patient but exacting teacher amenable to becoming the easterly version of a West Coast garden —a tangle of thick, floriferous growth, much of it in shade. My second Ontario home, where I live now, is higher and drier and windier with less soil, but my "internal garden" has modifed only slightly. This garden may have harsher lessons to teach, but this time, I intend to be a more joyful student.

That man is richest whose pleasures are the cheapest.
—Henry David Thoreau, 1856

All our gardens are expressions of what we were, tempered by what we are, what we have and what we want. "A garden is a mirror of the mind," wrote Maine gardener Henry Beston. This mirror of what we think, need and hope for may not always contain plants, and it need not be outdoors. The most sophisticated indoor garden may be the Japanese *knoiwa* or *tokoniwa*, a miniature landscape that can be as small as a dessert dish, popular where there is no space for an outdoor garden. Gardeners—and gardens—must bloom where they are planted, to paraphrase a poster of the 1970s.

The gardens I enjoy most are ones that are distinctly the creations of their owners, and the essays at the ends of the chapters are meant to help those people who want to make their gardens themselves. I find homemade gardens most relaxing if their owners do not expect ornamental plants to be all the same height, the same colour and in neat rows. I had teachers who expected their students to be like that. Trying to mould plants, sculpt them, carve trees into globes and set bedding plants at precise intervals in immaculate soil involves endless labour, which can be fun if you like that sort of thing but is more likely to lead to frustration. Gardening too easily becomes a contest of wills. Once you bring out the insecticides and the herbicides, gardening starts to feel like war.

I am impressed by gardeners who don't panic about weeds, although it seems that weeds do not take over their gardens. I am impressed by gardens that allow visitors to linger, with maybe a bench or chairs. These gardens may be spectacular in spots and at certain times of the year, or they may not. What they offer is adventure and a sense of calm and welcome. Some of my favourite gardens have areas that are quite messy. The most horticulturally adventurous people I have met have tended to have gardens in which some experiment is always going on, often many experiments, half of them threatening to take over where others leave off. Elizabeth Lawrence, whose writing was as passionate and generous as her North Carolina garden, once complained: "I cannot help it if I have to use my own well-designed garden as a laboratory, thereby ruining it as a garden." These gardens may add little to the resale value of the houses they accompany—a bottom-line reason for investing money in the landscape—but they are very clearly not there to impress potential buyers. Gardens that combine messiness with order, or experimentation with stability, are also probably the most fun.

As for recreating if a man be wearied with over-much study (for study is a wearinesse to the Flesh as Solomon by experience can tell you) there is no better place in the world to recreate himself than a Garden, there be no sence but may be delighted therein.
—William Coles, The Art of Simpling, *1656*

I like places in a garden where things look as though they have been that way for a while, maybe years and years. Very settled parts of gardens can be supremely peaceful. So can places waiting to be planted. Artist Robert Dash writes: "If my soul is messy, it is not entirely chaotic. . . . Somewhere I always have a patch of bare, newly tilled earth, like canvas bare and shining, to stay on centre. And I do plan the unexpected. Curved paths may follow crooked ones, but there are orderly straight walks as well."

What gardeners need in order "to stay on centre," as Dash says, is to keep the garden small enough or untended enough that we can take from it mostly enjoyment and give mostly what we can happily give. Our gardens are there to grow along with us.

As I worked my way through the chapters of this book, I realized that my problem in my previous garden came from concentrating not on what my garden had but on what it was missing. I was seeing its plants as though they were a collection of postage stamps in an album. I was not seeing the whole thing, the gestalt, from the sky above it to the bedrock below it and the boundary around it. I was not seeing the garden as a living, dying, dynamic blend of art, science and human history.

Our gardens are expressions of ourselves. They can be things we create and maintain by ourselves. The garden's walls mark the

15

boundaries of our private influence on the outdoor environment. Its paths lead us out into the world or lead us home. But more than that, our gardens are linked to ourselves by all the things that give us life, from the air we breathe to the water we drink, from the light that enables us to see to the warmth that allows us to move. The garden's rocks and soil are made from the same minerals that make our bones strong. Its plants live and die in a way that complements our living and dying.

What I wanted to do with this book was consider not just our remembered gardens, our future gardens and the gardens of our religions and legends—the internal gardens that impose themselves upon the real ones we tend and fuss over, curse and enjoy—but also the physical garden and the scientific basis that ties it to us. Albert Einstein wrote: "Where the world ceases to be the stage for personal hopes and desires, where we, as free beings, behold it in wonder, to question and to contemplate, there we enter the realm of art and of science." This science is so astounding and so essential to our lives that it puts into its proper perspective our fear that the petunias are in the wrong place.

When we see the garden as a blend of art and science, history and dreams, it can be an unencumbered source of wonder and joy.

On Light

When is my garden not a garden? On an overcast night maybe, the kind of night so dark that I slip off the path, scratch my arms on the rose thorns and snare my toes in the tomato cages. In that kind of darkness, the garden is so uninviting, it might as well not be there. Where I live, I should add, there are no streetlights, and my garden doesn't have any kind of artificial illumination, except for one light that is triggered by sound when someone approaches. That light guides me along the path to the house and then shuts off, closing the curtains on the small bit of garden it briefly lit. Then, the only light is what comes from the house windows to outline the shapes

19

of a few shrubs. The garden is primarily a visual experience, a feast for the eyes, so for me, it is little more than memory and expectation until it receives the light of the sun, moon or stars.

More than two-thirds of human sense receptors are in the eyes, so I am not alone in my dependence on light. Vision, more than any other sense, makes us feel safe as we move through the world. Whatever our culture, we have paid homage to the sun, stars and fire, which radiate light, and to the moon and all the colours that we see, which reflect light.

Truly the light is sweet, and a pleasant thing it is for the eyes to behold the sun.
—*Ecclesiastes 11:7*

Past generations imagined that almost all nature shared the human veneration of radiated or reflected light, not realizing there could be any other kind. When the sun rose in the morning, birds began to sing, bees and butterflies took to the air and flowers opened their petals. As the days lengthened after the winter solstice, animals gave birth and plants resumed growing, reaching toward the light, flowering and fruiting. There was no reason for people to think that anything other than beautiful, visible light woke the world every morning and every spring.

Darkness was the opposite. With dusk and autumn, the world fell helplessly away from the dominion of the sun. In the darkness, people lost their way, plants grew pale, the world became quiet, and many animals slept. Darkness was a dimly marked slate, a time to await the return of the light.

The biblical pronouncement "Let there be light" is echoed by gods and goddesses around the world. Light—sunlight, moonlight, starlight, firelight—is virtually synonymous with stories about the beginning of the world, the dawn of creation. This is the first day, the first rising of the sun. If not a god itself, such as Shamash, Mithra, Ra, Helios or Sol, then the sun was associated with a deity. So was the moon. The ancient Egyptians believed that the sun and moon were the eyes of the god Horus. When he opened his eyes, the universe filled with light. To Akhenaton, who was an Egyptian pharaoh around 1400 B.C., there was only one god, represented by the sun and depicted with rays terminating in human hands. The Incas believed that they were descended from Inti, the sun. The first light of creation dispelled the darkness that represented the void, or chaos, and in an instant brought into being time, hope and possibility. Suddenly, the universe could see its way.

If light seemed to be an improvement over darkness, then it was good, and all things good were associated with it. This metaphorical light illuminates the darkness of mystery and confusion. The Greek poet Pindar said of Apollo, god of light, "He is the god who plumbs all hearts, the infallible, whom neither mortals nor immortals can deceive either by action or in their most secret thoughts." Jesus called himself the light of the world. Buddha's very name means the enlightened one. He and the Christian saints and angels were actually said to glow. According to a 17th-century philosopher, a few

The sun, on account of the mist, had a curious sentient, personal look, demanding the masculine pronoun for its adequate expression.
—Thomas Hardy, Tess of the D'Urbervilles, *1891*

special, saintly mortals also had visible auras: those of doctors were green; those of nuns were white. The Inuit word *qua*, light, is also part of the words "forehead" and "knowledge."

The stone lanterns in some Japanese gardens represent the light of knowledge beaming into the darkness of ignorance. Unlike the brilliant, coloured night lights western gardens sometimes suffer, which Eleanor Perényi criticizes as "false dawns among the shrubs," the light from these grey lanterns is subtle enough to complement its partner the moon but bright enough to guide visitors along the garden paths when the moon does not shine.

The human association of darkness with such negative qualities as ignorance and evil arises from our dependence on eyesight. In reality, night is a time of regeneration, healing and growth. Roots do most of their growing by night. Many seeds germinate only in darkness, though they require light as soon as they sprout. Also, many plants measure the length of the night in order to gauge when to begin the process of flowering. Only a generation ago, one group of plants was known as "short-day" and another as "long-day," because it was assumed that their tendency to flower at a certain time of year was tied to day length. Then it was discovered that it was not the length of day but the length of night that mattered. If the darkness was interrupted with certain frequencies of light, the plant was thrown off schedule. This can be seen in shade trees that are planted under streetlights; they keep their leaves longer in fall than those growing in unbroken nighttime darkness. It also happens to chrysanthemums, which have been sold from Mother's Day to

Christmas since the discovery that they are short-day—actually long-night—plants. Before they will bloom, they require at least 15 uninterrupted hours of darkness in every 24, a schedule that can be provided any time of year in a greenhouse.

If darkness can be as potent as light, so can light that is not visible to our eyes. Scientists are now able to measure radiation that people can't normally see: the wavelengths that are above and below the visible arc of the rainbow. The discovery of all this unseen radiation gave new significance to the power of the words "let there be light" and to the centuries-old granting of the name of the Roman goddess of the rainbow, Iris, to the coloured membrane around the pupil of the human eye. The sun radiates frequencies of light that are crucial for life yet escape both the rainbow Iris and the human iris. Beyond the visible red is infrared, whose wavelengths, sensed as warmth, are too long for human eyes to perceive. Beyond visible purple is ultraviolet radiation, whose wavelengths are too short. There is also light that would be visible were it not absorbed into the objects it strikes, including ourselves. Desert dwellers have traditionally worn light-coloured clothing because it reflects most light, leaving them relatively cool. Dark objects, on the other hand, absorb most light.

O God, who is the true Sun of the world
always rising and never setting,
who, by your appearance, nourishes and gladdens
all things in heaven and earth,
We ask you to shine into our hearts
so that the night and darkness of sin
and the mists of error will be driven away
by the brightness of your shining within our hearts.
—*Erasmus, 1467-1536*

What people could not realize centuries ago was not only that the world becomes visible in the light—which is sufficiently miraculous to occupy anyone's imagination—but that light is necessary, directly or indirectly, for virtually all life. Almost a century ago, botanist G.F. Scott Elliott wrote: "All the work which we do with our brains or muscles involves the consumption of food which has been formed by plants under the warm rays of the sun. So that man's thoughts and labour, as well as that of every living creature, is in the first instance rendered possible by sunshine." Biologist Brian Capon puts it in 20th-century terms: "Autotrophic [photosynthesizing] plants hold the key to life on Earth; they alone are the intermediaries between the sun and all other creatures."

Green plants are a physical manifestation of light. By the process of photosynthesis, they use the energy of light to split water into its component parts: hydrogen and oxygen. The oxygen is released into the air, and the hydrogen is combined with atmospheric carbon dioxide to form carbohydrates—the cellulose, starches and sugars that fuel themselves, ourselves and all living things.

The chief substance in plants that is responsible for photosynthesis is chlorophyll, the pigment that colours most leaves and stems green. Chlorophyll is held within chloroplasts, which tend to cluster at the sides of cells closest to the light. When light levels rise above a certain point, the chlorophyll emits tiny electric currents that are harvested, used to split water molecules and to form an energy-rich compound which the plant can use immediately or store for later.

Among the flowers a pot of wine,
I drink alone; no friend is by.
I raise my cup, invite the moon
And my shadow. Now we are three.
—Li Bai, 701-762

Some orange pigments, carotenoids, are also photosynthetically active, but only chlorophyll can carry out the entire process. The carotenoids—which are responsible for the colour not only of their namesake carrots but also for such a diverse array of things as red tomatoes, green avocados and yellow autumn leaves—are also responsible for the human retina's sensitivity to light. From carotenoids in food, animals—including humans—synthesize vitamin A, which fuels our own light sensors. That old bit of advice about eating carrots for better vision has a basis in truth. One of the first symptoms of vitamin A deficiency is night blindness. Just as the moon illuminates by redirecting the sun's light, so can our eyes see the night garden through the power of the sunlight we have tapped into by eating carotenoids.

Both carotenoids and chlorophyll use light that the plant has absorbed, not reflected. Carrots look orange because they are absorbing blue-green light and reflecting the orange. Most leaves look green because green light is almost useless to them. Shine a green light on a plant in a dark room, and it will grow leggy and pale and die. What chlorophyll wants, mostly, is red and blue light, two of light's primary colours. Grow an indoor plant under a regular incandescent bulb and a cool blue fluorescent, which emit a lot of red and blue respectively, and the plant will survive. Green, the third primary colour of light—unlike the primaries of pigment, which are red, blue and yellow—is chlorophyll's garbage, thrown back at the world for any eyes that want it.

As ours do, of course. Green is one of the most restful colours for humanity. "He maketh me to lie down in green pastures....He restoreth my soul," says the most repeated of all psalms, the 23rd. In centuries past, engravers who had to do very detailed work often kept a green gemstone nearby at which they could gaze to rest their eyes. "Eye-ease green" was a shade developed for hospitals in Great Britain in the 1930s, and it is still used in operating and waiting rooms. Fuelled by light, plants produce not only the oxygen that allows us to breathe and the carbohydrates that feed us and the vitamin A that allows us to see but also the colour green that feeds our hungry souls.

Thus we decorate our homes and our shopping malls with leafy tropical plants—real or not—and we grow gardens wherever we can. It is in part the lovely tempering of light by foliage that makes lawns so welcome, whether by the square foot or the acre. Lawn grasses are about the easiest plants we cultivate, yet they reward us with an almost ceaseless show of green. Katharine White was garden columnist for *The New York Times* when she wrote that a lawn is "as changing and spellbinding as the waves of the sea, whether flecked with sunlight under trees of light foliage like elm and locust, or deep, dark, solid shade, moving slowly as the tide, under maple and oak. This carpet! What pleasanter surface on which to walk, sit, lie or even to read Tennyson?"

The green light under shade trees has been appreciated in gardens for much longer. More than 2,000 years ago, Pliny the Elder wrote that plane trees (*Platanus orientalis*) were being imported into Rome because they were so loved for their shade. A huge one owned by Licinius Mucianus sheltered a banquet of 18 people. After the banquet, Mucianus went to sleep in the tree, "shielded from every breath of wind," reports Pliny, "and receiving more delight from the agreeable sound of the rain dropping through the foliage than gleaming marble, painted decorations or gilded panelling could have afforded."

But if the green light that dapples a park bench under a canopy of maples is balm to the human spirit, it is a meagre diet for plants.

Look at an individual leafy plant or a community of plants from overhead, and you will see a foliage pattern that takes advantage of every ray of sunlight. Plants growing under a leafy canopy receive light whose useful red and blue wavelengths have already been gathered by the leaves above. The top layer absorbs about 90 percent of the visible radiation that contacts it, while the lower layers receive successively smaller amounts. Tulips that shrink and finally cease to appear in spring in what seems to be a perfect spot under the pine boughs have probably starved from too little light, just as surely as the trumpet vine planted in the deep shade on the north side of the house will. Many of the plants native to temperate deciduous woodlands, such as trilliums and hepatica, are appropriately called ephemerals; their season of growth and flowering is the short time after the soil thaws

A leaf is a subtle thing, being far more than a casual first appearance of form and colour and light. There are leaves which by their shape hold the light as in a cup, others which let it flow from them almost as rain might flow; there are leaves which are mirrors reflecting the sun from a glaze of varnished green, and others which are delicate transparencies through whose living screen the sun passes with a strange and lovely tempering.
—Henry Beston, Herbs and the Earth, *1935*

and before the trees above leaf out. Even their foliage may then quickly disappear. Some of them have seeds, too, that require red light to germinate and will stay dormant as long as they are bathed in green light from leaves overhead.

The lowest known light levels in the open air on Earth are on the floor of tropical rainforests. Plants that can survive there, such as philodendron, croton and peperomia, make ideal houseplants because they are accustomed to dim light year-round. In fact, their adaptations to this relatively gloomy world may enhance their visual appeal in the living room. They may produce large leaves that are high in chlorophyll, hence dark green, and they may augment their ability to absorb light with accessory pigments which give them additional colours. These species carry on their life processes slowly and cannot survive exposure to full sun.

Seaweeds live in a similar situation, a sort of aquatic forest whose light is filtered not by leaves but by water. The green plants that grow in garden ponds tend to keep their leaves close to, upon or even above the water's surface. Deeper down, where the light is more blue-green, algae are often brown or reddish, so they are able to make use of this filtered light. The clearer the water, the deeper plants can grow, but eventually, even in the clearest water, there is too little light for photosynthesis. Blue or blue-green light is also the type most able to penetrate snow, so some photosynthesis can continue under a blanket as deep as 80 centimetres (32 inches). Blue light also makes its way into soil more effectively than red light, though no light penetrates far, a boon to seeds that require darkness—a blanket of soil—to germinate.

Within all the greenery of the garden—and most gardens are mostly greenery in varying hue—there are apt to be many other colours, of course, that are of fleeting duration but as cherished as jewels. They flare and die like fireworks in slow motion. These colours are usually provided by flowers. Again, what the human eye sees is reflected light, but the colour reflected by flowers has a purpose. It is not simply rejected light, like the green of hostas or lawn grass. It is light geared to the visual sensitivity of the desired pollinator. White flowers, for instance, bounce back all the light that shines on them and so they show up best in dark places or in the evening. Moonflowers (*Ipomoea alba*), evening primrose (*Oenothera* spp), jasmine (*Stephanotis floribunda*) and four-o'clocks (*Mirabilis jalapa*) are among the white flowers that attract night-flying hawkmoths, whose eyes are sensitive to luminosity but are not especially adept at focusing. In an Arizona experiment, hawkmoths were observed visiting progressively lighter-coloured flowers as dusk fell and foraging almost exclusively in white flowers after nightfall. In the light of dusk, flowers of the evening may be almost as brilliant as the moon. The famous all-white garden at Sissinghurst was "cool with lilies and white roses and grey-foliaged plants on a summer evening," wrote Vita Sackville-West.

Moonlight is, of course, reflected sunlight, but this one generation of removal from direct radiation, with only 7 percent of the power of the sun, makes an enormous difference in the appearance of the garden. The human eye cannot see colour in moonlight, so the garden becomes a study in black and white. "The sun is god" is said to have been the dying sentiment of the British artist Joseph Turner. Certainly for any landscape artist—as it is for any garden designer—the sun is the governing influence, from the low, pale sun of winter to the high, bright sun of summer, and from the golden light of morning through the white light and deep shadows of noon to the pink of evening. Moonlight illuminates only what landscape designers call the garden's bones, its most obvious features. In *Green Thoughts: A Writer in the Garden*, Eleanor Perényi writes: "To see things in black and white is to see the basics, and I would now recommend to any designer of gardens that he go out and look at his work by the light of the moon." Louise Beebe Wilder felt, on the other hand, that the moon shed a forgiving light on the gardener's efforts: "The moonlit garden is the perfected creation—all our dreams come true. Whatever of beauty we have longed for, striven for in our gardens is graciously vouchsafed. There is no disturbing lie, not an imperfect group, not a petal out of place."

Colours change; in the morning light, red shines out bright and clear and the blues merge into their surroundings, melting into the greens; but by evening the reds lose their piquancy, embracing a quieter tone and shifting toward the blues in the rainbow. Yellow flowers remain bright, and white ones become luminous, shining like ghostly figures against a darkening green background.
—Rosemary Verey, The Scented Garden, *1981*

For those of us gardeners who are learning to accept the inevitability of petals out of place, there are more positive things to think about, in any case, when the garden is fully revealed and all imperfections made plain by the sun. Most pollinators work by day, and happily, we have much the same colour vision as they do, because it is for them, not us, that the flowers shine. Martha R. Weiss, a biology student at the University of California, writes: "Through [colour] signals, plants are able to play a surprisingly active part in their interactions with animals."

Hummingbirds search above all for the red of flowers such as salvia and fuchsia, and I have even seen them tap their long beaks against red Christmas lights left out past winter. Day-flying moths see a rainbow of colours, and so do bees. The bee's visual world includes at least 10 shades of ultraviolet too. Bees cannot detect the the bright red of certain poppies and portulaca but visit the flowers anyway because they reflect ultraviolet. Yellow petals and many blues also reflect ultraviolet strongly, but white petals reflect less.

Vita Sackville-West grew several narrow-spectrum gardens, including one with predominantly purple flowers, such as lavender, alliums and salvia. Although the human visitors to Sissinghurst are

27

impressed by the blues, the bees are probably drawn mostly to the secret ultraviolet reflected by these flowers. If our eyesight were slightly different—people who have had cataracts removed can appreciate this, because they can see some ultraviolet—we might call this the ultraviolet garden. "I loathe bees myself," wrote Sackville-West, "one single sting sufficing to send me to bed, quite seriously ill, for nearly a week. Yet I must admit to a romantic feeling for this self-contained world of little creatures, with their extraordinary arrangement of a life entirely their own but, at the same time, dependent upon what we elect to grow for them." Stripes and patterns on petals that are subtle or invisible to us may shine with an almost three-dimensional quality when the ultraviolet light reflected from them is made visible to human eyes under black light. Suddenly, we see what the bees see.

We are the stars which sing.
We sing with our light;
We are the birds of fire.
We fly over the sky.
Our light is a voice;
We make a road
For the spirit to pass over.
—Algonquin Song of the Stars

The all-blue garden at Sissinghurst was missing a few of the most popular flowers—dahlias, roses, tulips, begonias—for a good reason. None of these flowers is coloured blue by nature. Colours other than blue are better at attracting the right pollinators. But we humans have our demands too. Plant breeders have worked feverishly to fill in the gaps and have triumphantly produced the odd bluish rose that looks starved for oxygen.

The appearance of the garden is so important to us that we alter its occupants endlessly to be more pleasing to our sight. Mostly, we want bigger and brighter, and we want what nature cannot do. The flowers that bloom just for us are our servants, some beautiful and some strange, with colours and shapes that may bear little resemblance to anything recognizable by a honeybee or hawkmoth. Petunias, for instance, are by nature restricted to a colour range of white through blue and rose and lack the enzyme needed to create red. Horticulturists produced a red version in the 1980s by splicing in a gene from corn. Many more unnaturals, such as black tulips—actually a very dark purple because of concentrations of red or purple pigments called anthocyanins—are highly sought after too, if oddly so. The tulip 'Queen of Night,' which I think looks blighted or dying when it grows in a garden, is called in one catalogue "a striking flower of deep velvety maroon-black. Outstanding amongst brighter colours." The anomalies that have been created in the quest for these peculiar goals either look very much like other flowers—the breakthrough white marigold, for instance, could pass for a chrysan-

themum—or are as freakish as cats bred for hairlessness. 'Sunspot,'
a squat sunflower with a big head, has the grace of a lollipop.

But seed catalogues are filled every year with new colours and
new shapes, new visual attractions for our gardens. Food plants are
as susceptible as flowers. Red vegetables, from lettuce to cabbage,
have their followers, as do tomatoes streaked with orange and beets
that reveal concentric white rings when they are cut across. Stokes
has a collection of variously hued bell peppers they have named for
birds, including 'Redwing,' 'Canary,' 'Blue Jay,' 'Dove' and 'Black-
bird.' Red apples are so important to shoppers that some plant
breeders have gone to great lengths to come up with a bright red
version of 'Jonagold,' a perfectly acceptable apple in every respect
except for the golden blush on its skin. Roger Way, breeder of 'Jonagold,' says, "Americans eat with their eyes."

Successful gardeners—the ones whose thumbs we say are green,
as green as chlorophyll—cannot help gardening with their eyes. In
fact, they must learn how to work with what they see—and even,
by an extension of the imagination, with what they cannot see.
These gardeners who learn the importance of both light and darkness become like the depiction of Horus, the sun, whose rays were
arms that terminated in human hands. In their care, gardens shine,
day and night, with the borrowed beauty of the sun and moon.

In Light, In Shade

My garden faces south and east, which means that during the daytime, most of it is almost always in the sun. During the three years I
have lived here, my garden has been quietly and efficiently making
its own plant selections, choosing, in effect, plants that can tolerate
plenty of light—and its companions, heat and drought. When I am
on vacation, this selection process happens with an often dismaying
thoroughness. If I am away for three weeks during the summer and
little rain falls, all the plants that need frequent watering die. What
I have left when I return are plants that can tolerate drought and a
lot of sun. If I am away in the fall when we have frost, plants that
are frost-tender will die. When I come back, the hardy plants are
left. If I am away too much, the garden will not need me at all.

This could be an expensive and wasteful way of choosing which
plants are suited to my garden. It isn't, though, because most of
what I have was donated to me, brought from my last garden or

chosen for its suitability for this spot and has survived. I am also careful about hardening off, which is even more important than usual in a sunny place. Hardening off is the process of acclimatizing plants to a new environment, especially seedlings or houseplants moved outdoors. It must be done gradually, over several days and using outdoor shade at first, because plant tissues accustomed to the relatively dark conditions indoors can burn and die in the sun.

In Nature, broadly speaking, we find that red and scarlet and yellow are rare, given to us as stimulants, as vivid experiences. They are confined to sunset and sunrise skies, to autumn foliage and to flowers; while the "restul and reparative colours"—blue, green and violet, as revealed in the sky, the sea, the distance and the great green setting of grass and trees—make up the beautiful commonplace of our daily seeing.
—*Louis Beebe Wilder,* Colour in My Garden, *1918*

The garden that is evolving here is largely one of young trees—shade-to-be—as well as shrubs; drought-tolerant, self-seeding annuals, from petunias to poppies and cosmos; and a selection of perennials and biennials, ranging from spring bulbs and various violas that take advantage of the wet spring soil to tough sun lovers such as dianthus, gaillardias, echinaceas, chrysanthemums, achilleas, artemisias, sedums and *Stachys lanata.* Many of these perennials have the greyish leaves that are characteristic of a host of sun-loving plants. The grey colour comes from small hairs that help reflect the sun's light.

My previous garden was almost the opposite in orientation, though it is only a 10-minute drive from here. Much of it faced north or northwest. It was surrounded by tall pines that provided moving shade most of the day. The soil was deep and full of clay and seldom needed watering. Virtually everything I planted grew in that marriage of sun and shade, though in the darkest places, I depended upon plants known to tolerate little light: *Vinca minor,* ornamental grasses, evergreen shrubs and annuals such as impatiens, begonias, coleus and summering houseplants. That garden, too, was self-selecting.

Every nursery, every seed packet, every how-to-garden book will tell the gardener which plants are best suited to which sort of light. The information is easy to come by, but there are always surprises. I had not thought of dianthus, for instance, as tolerant of sun, but after one summer vacation, both 'Telstar Picotee' and 'Ideal Violet,' grown from seed and planted in a dry, west-facing bed, were among the greenest things that greeted my return.

Both of my gardens have been in temperate rural Ontario. Gardeners in cities will think that my definition of shade—the space near tall trees—is too easy. Where walls block the light all day, often the case in some spots in city backyards, almost nothing will grow except a few weedy grasses, and this is a good place for the decorative use of stone. Pots of plants can be moved from one side of the house in the morning to the other in the evening, taking advantage of whatever light there is.

The sunniest places far to the south of my Ontario garden, on the other hand, are suitable for cacti and succulents, plants naturally suited to bright, hot sun. Cacti are adapted to such a bright environment that their stems are the organs which accomplish photosynthesis; their leaves have been reduced to spines.

The appearance of plants thus offers clues to their suitability for light or shade, but in all cases, left to its own devices, the garden will make the final selections.

On Air

I n his 1962 book *The Education of a Gardener*, Russell Page, one of the world's best-known landscape designers, described an imaginary garden in an unusual way, in terms of the air: "Like clouds moving across the sky dissolving and reforming, now in towering round masses, now in long streamers or curling wraiths, now jagged and torn or neatly spread in fish-scale patterns over the sky, my garden's patterns shape and reshape themselves."

Air, like the garden it occupies, is always changing. Fluid just as water is, air occupies space, and it flows. In the garden, the air is most noticeable when it flows quickly, as wind, or when it is carrying visible things such as falling leaves or dandelion seeds or dust or snowflakes or butterflies. I notice it, too, when it carries invisible things, such as sounds that enter my ears, pollen and spores that make me sneeze, pollutants that irritate my eyes or the fragrances and odours that enchant and repel me.

The air makes the sky blue, creates the colours of sunrises and sunsets and carries all the sounds of the garden. Eleanour Sinclair Rohde writes in *The Scented Garden*: "To me, the loveliest music of the world is the music of the evening breeze in the lime-trees on a July evening. Each one of us, I suppose, dreams their own dreams and reads their own thoughts in the wondrously varied music of trees." For my family, this music comes from huge Carolina poplars that surround the house. The sound of the leaves in a summer breeze is like the clatter of pouring rain on a shingled roof. The garden is full of its own versions of Aeolian harps, harps designed to be set on a window ledge and played by the wind flowing over the strings.

Thus this Earth resembles a great animall or rather inanimate vegetable, draws in aethereal breath for its dayly refreshment and vitall ferment & transpires again grosses exhalations. And, according to the condition of all other things living, ought to have its time of beginning, youth, old age, and perishing.
—*Isaac Newton, 1642-1727*

Air fills the spaces between other things, making of our environment a kind of transparent consommé filled with more tangible substances. All terrestrial respiring things swim in the air—the invisible vapour, the soul, spirit, breath, aura, pneumatos of the world. Indirectly, the air joins every living thing to every other living thing in a ceaselessly moving web. It ties the present to the past. It joins all the gardens of the world with other gardens. My garden has whitefly, and soon, so does my neighbour's. The potatoes next door suffer from blight, and I await what is virtually inevitable. Gardeners know firsthand that life is not lived in a vacuum. Nor is any garden an island, for even islands become home to the windblown traces of other landmasses. The air over the mid-Atlantic carries the pollen of many plants, including oaks, alders, pines, plantains and grasses. New Zealand is a resting place for insects that have blown from Australia. Thanks to winds from the warmer south, Ontario has had unseasonable dragonflies in April. Aphids, thrips and scale, too, drift with the breezes.

The air is utterly honest, utterly egalitarian. For a time, it bears the traces of everything that happens within it and only needs to be captured and analyzed to tell its complex story. I light a match, start my car, sneeze or spray my apple trees, and countless molecules take to the air. We inhale carbon dioxide from the first furnaces of the Industrial Revolution and sulphur dioxide from smelters thousands of miles away. Everyone shudders, awaiting the fallout, when a nuclear bomb is tested in a distant corner of the world. A 1983 report from the Ontario Ministry of the Environment included this throat-burning brew of "suspected air pollutants and those ascertained as causing vegetation injury...fluorides, sulphur dioxide, ozone, peroxyacetyl nitrate, acid rain, boron, lead, chlorine, hydrogen chloride, arsenic, zinc, chromium, nickel, cobalt, salt spray, urea, nitrogen dioxide, ammonion, cement dust, magnesium-lime dust and soot."

At death, the material soul follows the body into the tomb; the aerial soul subsists free. The two souls survive and function in proportion to the physical and mental vigour they have acquired during life, through nourishment and study.
—Tzu-ch'an, 535 B.C.

No wonder the closed garden, *hortus conclusus*, was a cherished metaphor in ages past. A mediaeval author used the term to refer to the Virgin Mary. The only visitor allowed in this imagined garden, said the 17th-century writer, was "the Holie-Spirit, like a subtile wind." Many of us would close our gardens to all but the purest of winds if we could. But then, what passing delights would we shut out? What litter of blossoms from my neighbour's tree, what bees to pollinate the apples, butterflies to light on my honeysuckle or winds to set the leaves of the Carolina poplars fluttering? A summer wind strong enough to blow away mosquitoes is surely a merciful thing. Greenhouse gardeners know that a garden without enough air stagnates into a terrarium of moulds and, usually, rampant pests without predators.

Air scours out the garden. At the same time, the garden scours the air. In the 1980s, when the National Aeronautics and Space Administration (NASA) was searching for safe filtering systems for spacecraft, they found that plants could remove common indoor air pollutants, including carbon monoxide, nitrogen oxide, formaldehyde, benzene and trichloroethylene. More than a dozen houseplants were tested, and all had some beneficial effect. For instance, one large specimen of mother-in-law tongue (*Sansevieria laurentii*) was capable of cleaning the formaldehyde out of about 27 cubic metres (953 cubic feet) of indoor air in 24 hours. Indoor air is much more placid than outdoor air, but plants do their secret laundering outdoors too, one of many benefits of city trees.

More important, the air is fed by plants, and it is food for plants. Plants supply almost all of the atmosphere's oxygen, and they use the air's carbon dioxide in turn. People need oxygen, so plants are our inspiration in the most literal sense. If all plants were to die, we would soon gulp helplessly at the gas that surrounds us, like fish on the surface of a pond. All living things take some of what is in the air to create themselves.

Methinks, it should have been impossible
Not to love all things in a world so filled;
Where the breeze warbles, and the mute still air
Is Music slumbering on her instrument.
—Samuel Taylor Coleridge,
"The Aeolian Harp," 1796

The Earth's first living cells were anaerobic, like the ones that still bubble methane out of wet, airless places such as our lower intestines and the pits of outdoor privies. For the tiny creatures inhabiting such dank places, oxygen is poison. They have been hiding from the air for more than three billion years, ever since the birth of chlorophyll, green mother of most atmospheric oxygen. Now, the atmosphere is about one-fifth oxygen, a precariously correct proportion that will allow fires, including our internal fires, to burn, yet will permit a fire to be extinguished. About every 2,000 years, the air's oxygen supply is entirely renewed by plants. The bulk of the remainder of the air is nitrogen, and about one three-hundredths is carbon dioxide. The last proportion has almost doubled during this century because of the combustion of petroleum, natural gas and coal, which release molecules of the gas stored by plants millions of years ago. The proportion is expected to double again in the next 50 to 70 years, causing global warming and other climatic repercussions that can only be guessed at.

Chlorophyll uses light, water and carbon dioxide to create oxygen, among other things. It was the birth of this process—photosynthesis—that made possible the first gasp and cry of every infant born. Some of the oxygen created by centuries of photosynthesis became ozone, which is just as important to terrestrial life as atmospheric oxygen. The ozone forms a wispy layer at the upper edge of the atmosphere. There, this ethereal guardian angel absorbs the shortest rays of ultraviolet radiation, which would otherwise destroy the proteins in living cells. Lewis Thomas writes in *The Lives of a Cell: Notes of a Biology Watcher*: "You could say that the breathing of oxygen into the atmosphere was a result of evolution, or you could turn it around and say that evolution was the result of oxygen. You can have it either way. Once the photosynthetic cells had appeared, very probably counterparts of today's blue-green algae, the future respiratory mechanism of the Earth was set in place."

That environmental revolution aeons ago is recalled by many religions, myths and languages. According to ancient Chinese belief, the original limitless breath, *yuanqi*, issued out of the void at the beginning of time: "Its clear and pure elements rose lightly to form the sky; its heavy and gross elements coagulated to form the Earth." Phoenicians believed that *aer* was a pure substance, pure intelligence, while *aura*, breath, was the first living thing that proceeded from it. According to the book of Genesis, too, the creator and the created were united by air: "The Lord God formed man from the dust of the ground and breathed into his nostrils the breath of life, and man became a living soul." The respiratory mechanism of the Earth is called by the Hindus *prana*, meaning both life force and breath. The word *atman*, the Hindu universal soul from which all others arise, comes from the same Sanskrit root that led to a Greek word for breath, *atmos*. *Aer* can mean both air and breath in Latin as well as Greek and is the origin of "air" in English and *aire* in French. By extension, a piece of music called an air or an aria is one in which a voice or instrument takes wing, sometimes in solo flight.

Welcome, sulphur dioxide,
Hello, carbon monoxide,
The air, the air is everywhere.
Breathe deep while you sleep.
Breathe deep.
—G. Ragni and G. McDermott,
"Air," from the musical Hair

The air is universally perceived as the most mysterious component of life—invisible, yet more essential than food or water. Our first inhalation and last exhalation define the span of our lives. *Pneuma* is the Greek word for wind, breath and the Holy Spirit, the invisible member of the Christian trinity. Spirit, which comes from the Latin *spirare*, to breathe or blow, leads to the word inspiration, a creative force that comes from elsewhere, like the air. Spirit, too, is another word for ghost, the ethereal remains of a human being whose cumbersome body has been dropped like dust. Indeed, the ancient Greeks regarded the winds as spirits of the dead.

Air unites earthly humanity with heaven, home of the gods, who were said by the ancients to breathe ether, the purest air, the material that fashioned the stars. Until Albert Einstein proved otherwise, scientists theorized that ether was an unseen, weightless, undetectable substance that existed everywhere, even in a vacuum. The word ethereal suggests almost anything otherworldly. It also describes a certain group of fragrances, including that of pears.

Sweet fragrances are the invisible signatures of the most beneficent qualities of the air. Alchemists and physicians of past centuries believed that foul odours could cause illness and perfumes could heal. John Parkinson wrote in the 17th century: "That as many herbes and flowers with their fragrant sweet smels doe comfort, and as it were revive the spirits, and perfume a whole house; even so such men as live vertuously, labouring to doe good... doe as it were send forth a pleasing savour of sweet instructions."

No garden should go without at least one set of wind chimes—but there are wind chimes and there are wind chimes. Listen before buying is a sound rule.
—Allen Lacy, Allen Lacy's homeground, *Winter 1993*

The "pleasing savour" of the virtuous that Parkinson applauded was not only metaphorical. Saints reputedly smelled good; they had the odour of strawberries, according to one admirer with a good nose. An old Christmas carol I have sung asks, "Whence is that goodly fragrance flowing, stealing our senses all away?" the suggestion being that the source is the infant Jesus. Incense is burned in religious ceremonies to colour the air with an odour that becomes linked with the idea of sanctity. Part of the reason for the appeal of such perfumes, it has been postulated, is that in sensing them, we take long, deep inhalations and so relax ourselves the same way we would if we were meditating.

Fragrances are forever associated with certain experiences, because the sense of smell is the one most closely tied to our memories. "Children brought up amongst privet go into raptures of recollected infancy when they come across it in later years," writes British gardener Mirabel Osler. "It is an especially unique scent, and for us who don't have this association, it is hard to understand how fervour can be aroused by such a dim little leaf." For myself, the perfume of a litter of pine needles warmed by the sun brings blended memories of camping trips, picnics and Christmas trees and their associated feelings of excitement and peacefulness.

Most of our favourite perfumes come from the garden. The fact that plants create their perfumes for creatures other than us interferes not at all with our appreciation and use of them. It is our gain, this coincidence that fragrances meant to attract certain beetles, bees and moths attract us too, not only to the plants but also to one another. Some delicately perfumed day-blooming flowers are scented for the bees—honeysuckle, narcissus, apple blossom—while many of the evening bloomers such as nicotiana and datura are baited to attract moths. Beetle-pollinated flowers, from lily, elder and wild rose to skunk cabbage, have some of the strongest daytime odours, which may or may not be pleasing to our noses. Incidentally, the Greek word for beetle, *silphe*, led to the mediaeval term for spirits of the winds, sylphs. They befriended people who died chaste.

I prefer the harsh fragrance that rises from a slightly sinister or medicinal herb, supposedly poisonous, to that of the insipid elder or even to that of the privet, so sickly sweet and heavy that when in full flower it commands our respect along the lanes behind Cancale.
—*Colette,* Pour un herbier, *1949*

Plant breeders who worked long and hard to produce bigger, showier flowers but forgot about the scent finally responded to the outcry of gardeners, especially lovers of the rose. New roses nowadays are often fragrant. After all, if heirloom and wild roses bore flowers that were small and short-lived, they were nevertheless cherished, even venerated, because of their intoxicating perfume. One place modern breeders could look for a literal inspiration as well as for genetic matter is Bulgaria's cash crop of Kazanlik roses (*Rosa damascena trigintipetala*), a species that produces a distinctive odour to lure beetles and bees, which may or may not succumb in preference to, say, dandelions. But humanity is more faithful. Roses and lilacs were the favourite scents listed by 20,000 readers of *Omni* magazine in a 1986 survey. Attar, the essential oil of the rose, is valued at more than $2,000 a pound.

Perfume is to us sanctity, innocence, sexuality, worldliness, lust. To certain insects, it is irresistible, but who knows why? Do bees feel pleasure at the tug of a rose? What must it be like to slide one's entire body into the heart of *Rosa damascena*? Maybe bees sense only the need to go from point A, the hive, to point B, the rose, and back again, pulled to and fro like iron filings to a magnet by molecules of rose oil and honey. To imagine any more is to fill our world with sensual intent. In any case, we are lucky that our threshold of fragrance detection is about the same as that of the bee, pollinator of most garden flowers.

Plants use the air to send various types of fragrances, not just perfumes, and not just to attract. The herb plot is likely to be the part of the garden with the fewest insect problems, because the very flavours and odours that appeal to us are the plants' natural defences against creatures that might otherwise be tempted to munch. Like perfumes, these plant substances also come from essential oils. The Latin *esse*, meaning "to be," is the root of the word essence, which is, like breath or air, another way of suggesting the spirit or the most subtle extract of something.

...the Body feeds upon Meats...be it twice a day or oftener: whereas, upon the Aer...it is always preying, sleeping or waking; and therefore, doubtlesse, the election of this constant and assiduous Food, should something concerne us, I affirme, more than even the very Meat we eat.
—*John Evelyn,* Fumifugion, *1772*

Essential oils that produce herbal odours may be capable of more than repelling foes. Some can kill. Experiments on bean weevils have shown that vapours from a virtual kitchen cabinet of herbs—lemon thyme, basil, sweet marjoram, rosemary, cumin, summer savory, thyme, sage, coriander and oregano—are all capable of killing more than half the insects within 24 hours. That is why grains have traditionally been stored with the leaves of aromatic plants, such as a bay leaf in a bin of flour.

Odours travel through the air not as waves, in the manner of sound or light, but in the much earthier form of molecules, which alight like butterflies in the mucosa of our noses. From there, signals pass to a primitive part of our brain. Those molecules tend to be heavy and thus to lie close to the ground. If you want to smell the flowers, grow them at nose level or bend to meet them or sit on the ground on a still summer morning the way children do. Never are odours so strong as then. The flowers for attar of roses are picked at dawn, because sometime in midmorning, the oil content in the petals begins a precipitous fall to about half the dawn level. Floral fragrances are complex, and some aspects may dissipate more quickly than others, so a flower may smell quite different in the morning than later on in the day. Bicycling along a country road early one tranquil July morning, my husband John and I passed through a succession of fogs of scent so strong they were almost visible. I could not identify them and can hardly describe them—musky and fresh, sweet and acrid—there are too few words to describe smells. Later in the day, we scarcely detected anything but the easily identifiable odours of hay, diesel fuel and cattle.

If the molecules of odour carried by the air can make us blissful or cause us to faint—as it is said the smell of some of the largest tropical carrion flowers can do—larger particles that plants send out on the air can cause sickness. Pollen is, in a sense, the plant's dusty sperm. Some of it never leaves the plant that produced it, and some is carried away by cooperative bees, flies, beetles and other riders of the skies. This pollen usually stays within about 15 metres (50 feet) of home, and thanks to the restricted diet of most insects, it has a good chance of reaching its target.

A lot more pollen is carried on the wind. Hay fever is a sign of pollen gone astray. It has ended up in a nose rather than on a stigma, which is the female plant organ. This is not a symptom of botanical failure, however, but a sign of the success of excess. Plants that use the winds unaided by flying insects produce lit-

11 July. A great gale.... All the Poppies by N. wall of house were laid flat along the path. Everything in the garden was leaning desperately toward the west. A giant leafy bough had plunged off the old apple stump at end of W. veg. gdn. But the Delphiniums & Verbena & Foxglove stand fast.
—Elizabeth Smart, Elizabeth's Garden, 1989

eral clouds of lightweight pollen—about one million grains of pollen for each ovule, compared with 6,000 grains for insect-pollinated plants—because the wind is an overzealous ally. Pollen has been found in midocean, and more than 5.5 kilometres (3.5 miles) above the Mississippi River basin. The strategy works; coniferous trees, for instance, have survived for at least 290 million years by casting their fate to the wind. The flowers of such plants are functional but not showy—the wind needs no beguiling—so gardeners who grow wind-pollinated plants, including most trees and grasses, do so for reasons other than floral beauty, though the combined effect of grassy seed heads can be eye-catching.

Trees produce their flowers and their clouds of smoky yellow pollen early, before their leaves grow and get in the way, but most grasses shed their pollen in late summer. This is hay fever season, although the worst culprit, at least in central and eastern North America, is not hay or, as was once believed, goldenrod, but common ragweed (*Ambrosia artemisiifolia*).

Fungal spores are another irritant. In Britain, where ragweed is uncommon, asthma and respiratory diseases are nevertheless troublesome in late summer; fungi are believed to be among the causes. These primitive plants, which are not capable of photosynthesis but live off the energy produced by green plants, release into the air their simple seeds, their spores—about 16 billion in a week from an

41

ordinary field mushroom (*Agaricus bisporus*). From July through September, fungal spores are far more numerous than pollen grains in the air over the garden. At three different sites in Pennsylvania, for example, a cubic metre of air (about 35 cubic feet) was found to contain 65,000 spores of the common mould *Cladosporium hermodendron* in an hour, compared with a maximum of 250 grains of ragweed pollen. (The average ragweed count was just 53, but that is not good news in itself, because hay fever can be triggered by only one pollen grain in a cubic metre.) The largest number of spores usually filled the air between midnight and six in the morning, but the peak could occur when a short rain shower was followed by a drop in humidity and an increase in wind. During a prolonged rainfall, the number of spores decreased, along with other airborne particles.

The supreme importance of respiration, being as it is one of the most universal and fundamental processes of living protoplasm, is recognized by all physiologists.
—*Walter Stiles and William Leach,* Respiration in Plants, *1932*

Airborne fungal spores cause most plant diseases too—the rusts, moulds, smuts, blights, rots and mildews that discolour, disfigure and sometimes kill. A century ago, John Tyndall called fungal diseases "vegetable parasites" and wrote that the air was responsible for carrying all kinds of objectionable "floating-matter," some harmful to people, some to plants. "If you see a new thistle growing in your field, you feel sure that its seed has been wafted thither. Just as sure does it seem that the contageous matter of epidemic disease has been sown in the place where it newly appears."

The seeds of thistles are among many that make use of the air to colonize new territory. Although the easiest way for a plant to spread its seeds is by gravity—the reason poppies and sunflowers sprout in much the same place where their parents grew last year—the technique has its drawbacks. It is fine for annuals, which can let their children inherit the earth, but the seeds of perennials are better off if they do not fall at the feet of the parent, where the situation may be too competitive for germination and healthy growth. Some plants catapult their seeds into the wind, while many others use messengers of independent motion, from birds to wool socks.

For gardeners, the success of seeds that travel on the air is apparent as "new thistles growing in your fields" and, more pressingly, as dandelions that are almost unstoppable. Goatsbeard, chicory and wild asters, too, are among the hundreds of plants whose seeds fly on fluffy parachutes beloved of children. For plants native to open ground and other windy places, this dispersal system is wide-ranging and obviously effective. The dandelion (*Taraxacum officinale*), an edible plant native to Europe, Asia and northwest Africa, now grows everywhere on Earth where the climate is suitable. And as if to enhance its plan to blanket the world, the dandelion produces parachutes designed to land at a 45-degree angle, all the better to bring the growing tip into contact with the ground, the best position for speedy germination.

Gardeners would do well to recapture their childhood appreciation of the generous dandelion, source of food, wine and colour, because it is as likely to remain in our gardens as the wind that brings it. The dandelion is a persistent reminder that the air gives and takes away and is the breath and life of our gardens and ourselves.

In the Lee

My family lives on the top of a hill, a great spot for views in all directions. Looking east or west over fields and forests, you feel as though you can see forever. And it is a great place for wind. The laundry tangles on the line, porch chairs topple, the empty watering can rolls down the driveway, and my garden dries out in minutes, it seems, on a hot day. These warm winds are, I suppose, the zephyrs, named for Zephyrus, west wind of the ancient Greeks.

Some plants seem unaffected by the zephyrs, but scientific assessments have shown that almost everything grows better with shelter on the windward side. A windbreak can help avoid soil erosion too, and it need not be tall or terribly close. Wind protection extends on the leeward side to a distance 8 to 10 times the height of the barrier. Permanent windbreaks include buildings, walls and fences. Living windbreaks, as tall as a line of Lombardy poplars or as small as a clump of flowers, are usually perennial, but annuals can also be useful.

When this garden was new to me, for instance, I sowed a row of burning bush (*Kochia scoparia*) seeds on the windward side of a nursery bed, a former sandbox filled with bulbs, rhizomes and chunks of perennials from my previous garden. Kochia is a fast-growing, drought-tolerant annual—so tough and fast-growing, in fact, that it is a noxious weed on the prairies, where hot winds discourage it hardly at all. It grew to its full height of about a metre (3 feet) in time to shelter the more delicate perennials from midsummer on, when drying winds were at their worst and temperatures were highest. In the meantime, I began to plant wind-tolerant perennials in strategic spots throughout the garden so that they could eventually protect other things. Even a plant the size of a day lily can provide shelter to smaller things nearby.

Many shrubs are wind-resistant and ideal for planting near a flower, herb or vegetable garden. Among the plants recommended by Agriculture Canada for hedges on the prairies—and therefore suitable for just about anywhere—are the following: caragana (*Caragana* spp), Siberian dogwood (*Cornus alba* 'Sibirica'), golden willow (*Salix alba* 'Vitellina'), redstem willow (*S.a.* 'Chermesina'), common lilac (*Syringa vulgaris*), euonymus (*Euonymus* spp), honeysuckle (*Lonicera* spp), bush cinquefoil (*Potentilla fruticosa*) and Saskatoon (*Amelanchier alnifolia*). These shrubs need not be planted in rows, of course. Single specimens or small groupings might be more decorative.

The beneficial effect of a windbreak on cultivated crops has been measured in terms of increased yield in tons per acre, but ornamental plants will also thrive, though in ways less easily measured. The advantages will be apparent not in economic terms but as untorn leaves, straight stems, long-lasting flowers and overall plant health. Perhaps best of all, the garden will be a pleasant, sheltered environment for its human visitors.

On Warmth

Fire and ice are all I really know, firsthand, about the hottest hot and the coldest cold. Fire and ice mark the boundaries of sensation, like the quietest and loudest sounds I can hear. The coldest cold is what I feel when I hold a snowball in my bare hand until it drips through my fingers. Anything colder causes pain, then cell damage and, finally, cell death. The hottest hot is what I feel when I sit at arm's length from my woodstove until the baking-wool smell of the back of my sweater alarms others in the winter living room. A worry it is for them—if I were much hotter, I would feel not heat but pain—but this woolly baking is utter pleasure for me. A certain spot in front of the stove

47

is my own private Palm Beach. When I am sitting there, I feel something like the tiny flies that biologist Roger Knutson observed gathering in the upturned pasqueflowers (*Anemone patens*) on a cool spring day. He found that the temperature within the cup of sun-warmed petals was about 10 Celsius degrees (18 Fahrenheit degrees) warmer than the air that surrounded it. "If you are small enough," he wrote, "Palm Beach is as close as your nearest pasqueflower."

Sprigs of plum by the corner of the wall
Are blooming alone in the cold;
If not for the subtle fragrance drifting over
Who could tell this from snow on the boughs?
—Wang Anshi, "Plum Blossom," 1021-1086

If Palm Beach for the gnats is as close as the petals of a sunny flower in cold weather and if Palm Beach for me is as close as my woodstove, Palm Beach for plants in the garden is as close as, well, Palm Beach. They cannot flee or fly to warmer places. They must endure the insults of the weather, and many are endowed with the ability to do so. A plant that can create its own little sauna, like the pasqueflower, can warm its pollen and ovaries and attract pollinators too, all the better to ensure fertilization. A plant's cells, in common with mine and those of all other living things, are mostly water and are at their best at a temperature somewhere about halfway between boiling and freezing.

It is not a huge temperature range, this span between snowball and simmer. It is a mere 100 degrees on the Celsius scale (180 Fahrenheit degrees), which plummets far below zero to absolute zero—minus 273.13 degrees (–459.63°F). Toward the high end is the temperature of the core of the sun at something like 15 million degrees (27 million°F). Given such almost unimaginable extremes, even the toughest cells—those that survive boiling ocean vents or Siberian winters—are fragile things which inhabit a delicate cusp between death and death. If any of us living things are too cold, we will become a solid. If we are too hot, we will become a gas. Even to approach gas or solid is to experience discomfort. On the other hand, bliss lies somewhere between the two extremes.

For me, the magical temperature of greatest comfort is around 25 degrees Celsius (75°F), just what I find on a perfect summer day in the garden, the kind of day that hints of the Elysian Fields, the Greek paradise. In fact, everybody who imagines heaven at all pictures it as a place of comfortable warmth. Even the Inuit of Baffin Island do. Their idea of hell is not fire, like ours, but ice. Like the trees in my garden in winter, the people of the Arctic endure bitter weather for now because they must, but they anticipate something considerably more comfortable in the life to come.

Gnats, pasqueflowers and gardeners alike, we await that magical, wonderful midrange of warmth that ends winter. The sun climbs higher in the sky after the December solstice, but we remain anxious until the weather actually warms up, a promise that crops will grow again. Increasing warmth lags behind increasing light because the air is heated not directly by the sun but by the earth, water and other things that must be warmed first. In May, when the weather remains

Always dark…no sun…snow flying all the time, terrible storms, cold, very cold, and a great deal of ice there.
—Inuit description of hell recounted on Baffin Island, 1862

stubbornly cool, the tropical annuals I have transplanted into the garden stay the same size for weeks—tomatoes, peppers, nicotiana, gazania and the like. They don't die unless there is a frost, but neither do they grow, and likewise, I'm not quite warm enough to sit comfortably on the porch. Then there comes a day when I can say, "The sun is hot." Birds are nesting, and every plant in the garden is springing forth, rambling and reaching and leafing out, and I am in a deck chair. I bask in the sunlight, enjoying the play of shade under the trees, smelling the garden's fragrances and hearing its hisses and buzzes. Everything is alive, all at once.

This time of perfect temperatures is what I anticipated all spring and will fondly recall all fall and winter. As far as I am concerned, this is the garden's finest hour. I have been encouraged by wiser gardeners to beautify my winter garden—not bad advice where winter, loosely defined, lasts a good half of the year—but my attempts to choose plants with colourful bark and graceful seed heads to look at through the frosty windows cannot lure me to sit out there on the slippery garden bench. A watering can I forgot to bring indoors has burst from swelling ice. Snow has drifted around one side of the bench, and the wind has scoured the snow away from the other side, exposing what looks like threadbare beige indoor-outdoor carpeting. The trees have shrunk to mere outlines of their summer selves. I, like my garden, wait for better weather. In temperate places, that means waiting for warmth.

For almost all living things, too much cold is a greater environmental danger than too much heat. The last frost of spring and the first frost of fall mark the boundaries of the gardening season more distinctly than any other dates. How much cold is too much? That varies. Otherwise all of our gardens, from the equator to the arctic circle, could look much the same, with a landscape of tea roses, pines, palms, magnolias and fruit trees ranging from apples to mangos.

Frost dates mean nothing but a change of internal gears to some plants, but they mean certain death to others. Some tropical plants are so vulnerable to cold that prolonged exposure to what northerners consider a lovely springtime temperature of 15 degrees C (59°F) can kill them. On the other hand, the Dahurian larch (*Larix dahurica*) can tolerate minus 65 degrees C (–85°F) during a Siberian winter, much colder than the temperature that will freeze the mercury in the thermometer. But even the larch can be killed by cold that challenges its ability to adapt. Robert Cook of the National Science Foundation in the United States writes that plants "respond to falling temperatures simply by slowing down cellular processes, which run about half as fast for every 10-degree [F; 5.5 Celsius-degree] drop. The slowdown cannot continue indefinitely, however; if temperatures drop below the point at which a particular plant can continue functioning, injury will result."

As our seasons vary from year to year, a fair degree of latitude must be granted anyone who attempts to classify either flowers or birds "according to season." But usually the same flowers are contemporaneous.
—*Mrs. William Starr Dana*, According to Season, *1894*

The map of climatic zones used throughout North America reflects the truth that plant growth is limited mostly by cold, not heat. The map is a patchwork quilt of zones, each of which has a number. The United States Department of Agriculture (USDA) system divides up all of North America, from the coldest stretches of the Arctic, called zone 1, to the hottest deserts of southern Mexico and the beaches of Hawaii, zone 11. These zones are defined exclusively by average minimum temperature, from a bone-numbing low of minus 45.6 degrees C (–50°F) for zone 1 to a rather pleasant low of 4.4 degrees C (40°F) for zone 11. No mention is made of maximum temperatures. The Canadian zone system also assigns lower numbers to areas with harsher winters but takes into account six additional climatic factors, one of which is summer heat. Most nurseries use one system for classifying plants, so gardeners who know which zone they are in know which plants to choose. My garden is in Agriculture Canada zone 5, USDA zone 4.

The zone maps are useful when they are matched up with perennial plants classified by their coldest zone of hardiness. Using climatic-zone designations to choose perennial plants thus becomes a bit like painting the garden by numbers. Most plants can survive in any zone with a higher number than their designation, but the reverse is seldom true, even to the extent of one zone down, because cold is so limiting to growth. I am in zone 5, so I should be able to grow plants Agriculture Canada considers hardy in zones 1 to 5, but I will be pushing my luck if I try anything assigned to zone 6 or above. I should be able to grow, for instance, American larch (*Larix laricina*), hardy in zone 1; 'Hopa' crab apple (*Malus* 'Hopa'), hardy in zone 2; redstem willow (*Salix alba* 'Chermesina'), zone 3; ginkgo (*Ginkgo biloba*), zone 4; and Kentucky coffee tree (*Gymnocladus dioicus*), zone 5. But my recklessness will increase exponentially with each of the following plants: Japanese cherry (*Prunus serrulata*), zone 6; English yew (*Taxus baccata*), zone 7; and Pacific madrone (*Arbutus menziesii*), zone 8.

Sometimes, in a summer morning, having taken my accustomed bath, I sat in my sunny doorway from sunrise to noon, rapt in a revery, amidst the pines and hickories and sumachs, in undisturbed solitude and stillness....I grew in those seasons like corn in the night, and they were far better than any work of the hands would have been.
—Henry David Thoreau, Walden; or, Life in the Woods, *1854*

If I lived in a city instead of on an exposed hilltop between dairy farms, I might give the Japanese cherry a try—and might even hazard the English yew in a protected corner. Climatic-zone indications are simply guidelines. Gardeners in cities enjoy relatively warmer conditions than the zone maps indicate. According to Richmond Longley of Agriculture Canada, "Heat from large cities tends to keep temperatures in the vicinity a few degrees higher than over the surrounding area, particularly on cool nights." Although cities receive less sunlight than the nearby countryside, their temperatures are 10 percent higher on average because they have more heat sources, such as automobiles and industry, and because they have more surfaces to reflect light and heat. Car tops and asphalt were found to reach a scorching 55 degrees C (131°F) on a summer day in Manhattan. At 8 p.m., the asphalt temperature was still a balmy 33 degrees C (91°F). This sort of heat not only warms the air but can actually damage nearby plants. The upper limit of heat tolerance before cell damage occurs in most plants is about 40 degrees C

(104°F). No wonder streetside trees must be tough as nails to survive not only winter's cold but summer's heat, as well as road salt, air pollutants, acid rain and acts of botanical vandalism.

Not only are there climatic differences within zones, but plants are not consistently hardy from seedling to old age or from tip to root. Many perennials become hardier with age; gardeners can only hope that young plants will not have to endure what horticulturists descriptively call a "test winter." Also, underground plant parts are designed to inhabit a gentler world than shoots and so are considerably less hardy than aboveground parts of the same plants. Frost heaving can kill plants simply by exposing their roots to the bitter air. Species that are normally hardy often die, too, if they are left in pots outdoors over winter, because they have too little soil insulating their roots. Recent research at Cornell University showed that young roots are particularly vulnerable. For instance, creeping juniper (*Juniperus horizontalis* 'Plumosa'), a plant that is rated hardy to USDA climatic zone 2—in other words, to an average winter minimum of about minus 45 degrees C (–50°F)—has young roots that can be killed at minus 11 degrees C (12°F), which is the equivalent of zone 8. The top of the plant can survive Skagway; the roots need Seattle. The roots of less hardy plants, such as tropical houseplants, have even less cold tolerance.

For love is gentle and love is kind,
The sweetest flower when first it's new,
But love grows old and waxes cold
And fades away like the morning dew.
—"The Water is Wide," folk song

It is easy to see why irrigation with cold water is never recommended, outdoors or in. Several centuries ago, John Parkinson wrote: "I would advise you to water none of your dainty flowers or herbes with any water that hath presently before been drawne out of a well or pumpe, but onely with such water that hath stood open in the Sunne in some cisterne, tubbe or pot for a day at the least, if more the better: for that water which is presently drawne out of a well, &c., is so cold, that it presently chilleth & killeth any dainty plant be it younger or elder grown, whereof I have had sufficient proofe: and therfore I give you this caution by mine own experience."

Plant roots, like burrowing animals and earthworms, enjoy the persistent ability of the earth, the skin of the planet, to maintain relatively comfortable temperatures under its surface—from desert to tundra and summer to winter. This is one of many reasons the ancients referred to the earth as Mother.

A plowed field in England in early September was found to have daily fluctuations of 15 Celsius degrees (27 Fahrenheit degrees) on the surface, but just 2 centimetres (0.8 inch) down, the daily range was only about half as great. Desert soil that is a scorching 60 degrees C (140°F) on the surface is 27 degrees C (81°F) just 20 centimetres (8 inches) down, near to my own standard of temperature perfection. Considerably farther down, 9 or 10 metres (30 to 33 feet) below the surface, the earth maintains a constant temperature of approximately 12 degrees C (54°F). This is a secret Palm Beach whose warmth is approached if not reached by deep roots and the builders of underground houses. Go deeper—in a mine shaft, say—and the temperature rises steadily the farther you descend.

This fall everyone looked to the bands on a woolly bear caterpillar and predicted as usual the direst of dire winters. This routine always calls to mind the Angiers' story about the trappers in the far north. They approached an Indian whose ancestors had dwelled from time immemorial in those fir forests and asked him about the severity of the coming winter. The Indian cast a canny eye over the landscape and pronounced, "Bad winter." The others asked him how he knew. The Indian replied unhesitatingly, "The white man makes a big woodpile."
—*Annie Dillard,* Pilgrim at Tinker Creek, *1975*

That deep heat comes from the geothermal furnace that is the Earth's molten core, but the surface heat is from the sun. Dark-coloured soil absorbs nearly four-fifths of the long-wave, heat-producing energy of the sun. A light-coloured sand absorbs about a third, so it heats more slowly and cools more quickly—like a cotton sheet as opposed to the wool blanket that is humusy soil. When I put my hand on a sunny patch of soil, even in early spring, I can feel its steamy warmth: breast of the earth goddess. The ancient Sabine people invoked the creative power of the fertility goddess Ops by pressing their hands against the earth on her festival day, December 19. For the ancient Greeks, longer days were a sign of the imminent return of Persephone, daughter of the vegetation goddess Ceres. Persephone would bring the warmth of the sun, and everything living would borrow the warmth of the sun's fire, passing it on like a sacred torch that keeps all cells alight.

I once had a soil thermometer—long since lost—so that I could measure the steady warming of the soil in spring just as I might take the temperature of a feverish patient. The thermometer was supposed to show me when to plant things, but it turned out to be more interesting than practical; after a few years, every gardener has a pretty good idea of when to plant what without resorting to a thermometer. What is fascinating, however, is watching the soil's hidden life awaken as it is sparked by the heat of the sun. Nothing much happens until the soil reaches about 5 degrees C (41°F), when the first weed seeds sprout. They are well on their way be-

The fire passes in flame and smoke, what was lovely green is now a deep black; the Rains descend, and this odious colour disappears, and is replaced by a still brighter green; if these grasses had not this wonderful productive power on which fire has no effect, these Great Plains would, many centuries ago, have been without Man, Bird or Beast.

—David Thompson describing the Great Plains, 1812

fore some of the hardy annuals such as cornflowers (*Centaurea cyanus*) and California poppies (*Eschscholzia californica*) germinate at 15 to 20 degrees C (59 to 68°F). As each temperature threshold is crossed, new species germinate, first in soil exposed to the sun, then later in shade. Surface seeds germinate earlier than deeper ones, bringing successive waves of the same species for weeks.

Meanwhile, insects appear, creatures that depend upon the sun's warmth to be able to move and mate. The thoracic muscles of winged insects must reach a certain temperature before they can fly; the minimum takeoff temperature for the bean aphid is 9 degrees C (48°F). This is why dragonflies rest on sunny rocks on cool days. There, they may be 10 Celsius degrees (18 Fahrenheit degrees) warmer than the air. Monarch butterflies normally do not appear until the air temperature is consistently above 10 degrees C (50°F).

The sliding scale of temperature that establishes the pitch for the symphony of life fascinated early scientists, especially as it concerned humans. More than 2,000 years ago, Hippocrates correlated what he considered the four elements of nature—air, earth, fire and water—with four humours, bodily substances, each of which had its own ballpark temperature. Blood was hot and wet like air; black bile was cold and dry like earth; choler was hot and dry like fire; and phlegm was cold and wet like water. The common cold was named according to this scheme.

Medicinal plants were classified as having hot or cold powers that complemented the diseases they could treat. Thus a mustard plaster—mustard being a hot plant—was considered a cure for a cold. Rosemary was another warm plant, according to 17th-century English physician Nicholas Culpeper: "The Sun claims dominion over it. The decoction of Rosemary in wine helps the cold distillations of rheums into the eyes, and other cold diseases of the head and brain." On the other hand, common nightshade was, wrote Culpeper, "a cool Saturnine plant...used to cool hot inflammations. The juice dropped into the ears eases pains that arise from heat or inflammation; it is good for hot swellings under the throat." Hippocrates summed up his feelings about temperature: "Cold is inimical to the bones, the teeth, the nerves, the brain and the spinal marrow, but heat is beneficial."

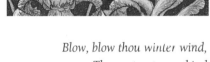

Many of the same people who followed the doctrine of the four humours believed that trees survived winter's cold by producing their own "vital heat." People imagined they could feel this heat— probably when they pressed their hands against bark warmed by the sun—and they must have been further fooled by a few rare plants able to muster a dramatic if temporary fever. The skunk cabbage (*Symplocarpus foetidus*), for instance, can warm itself as much as 35 Celsius degrees (63 Fahrenheit degrees) above the ambient temperature to melt through the icy ground of February or March and proffer its stinky inflorescence to pollinating beetles. Then it settles into the cold-blooded habits of all plants, warming in the sun and cooling under a cloud or at night. In winter, unlike the trees, it leaves nothing at all showing above the ground, one of the best and most popular botanical ways of avoiding the hardships of winter.

Blow, blow thou winter wind,
Thou art not so unkind
As man's ingratitude;
Thy tooth is not so keen,
Because thou art not seen,
Although thy breath be rude.
—William Shakespeare,
As You Like It, *1599*

If hiding in the relatively warm soil, all above-ground parts allowed to wither away, is an effective way for many plants to survive temperatures too low for growth, so is overwintering in the form of seeds. Temperate-world annuals, like tropicals, know nothing of winter. For them, the year begins in spring when the soil is warm enough for germination and ends after a few fall frosts. Thousands of the plants that are as much a part of summer as picnics—poppies, pigweed, mustard and ragweed, to name a few—endure ice and snow as seeds: tiny time capsules of genetic matter, some of them durable enough to last for centuries and to survive temperatures so low they can be encountered only in a laboratory. Biennials, a rarer group of plants that takes two years to grow from seed to fruition, overwinter alternately as seeds and as half-grown plants. The first spring, the seeds germinate and the plants grow fat, fleshy tap roots and rosettes or clumps of foliage close to the ground, a form that holds in the soil's warmth, escapes the wind and allows plants such as foxglove or hollyhock, parsley or parsnip to take advantage of the protection of taller plants and the snow.

For a winter garden, snow is a merciful thing, a kind of intermediary between the warm earth and the cold air. It is good for roots, and it is good for any above-ground plants that are low enough to be covered. It is good for the builders of igloos and snow caves. "Year of snow, fruit will grow," an old English proverb assures us. Snow is an efficient absorber of long-wave radiation from the sun and from objects around it such as trees, but more to the point, it is a good insulator. It acts something like a wet goose-down comforter or wet wool socks. Fresh snow is roughly one-tenth water fluffed up with nine-tenths air, so when its surface is exposed to a temperature of minus 30 degrees C (–22°F), the ground 2 metres (6.5 feet) below can be 0 degrees C (32°F)—not balmy but Californian enough to be tolerable for many plants that would swiftly die if exposed to the air.

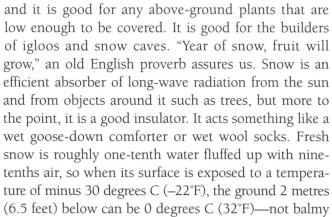

Sun, my relative
Be good coming out
Do something good for us.
Make me work.
So I can do anything in the garden
I hoe, I plant corn, I irrigate.
—*Havasupai prayer*

In my garden, snowfall is undependable, so I use a mulch to do some of its job. After leaf drop, I pile 8 to 10 centimetres (3 to 4 inches) of grass clippings and fallen leaves on my perennial beds. The mulch has to be pulled away from the plant tops when shoots begin to turn green in spring. Under deep snow or mulch, gardeners can grow plants that would otherwise be fantasies. In cold places like this, the only way gardeners can overwinter tea roses is by mounding them with soil or protecting them in cages filled with leaves or straw.

But no matter how much snow or mulch there is, some plants will stick up above it. Woody perennials protect themselves as best they can by undergoing a kind of constitutional revolution that goes right to their cells. First, they pare themselves down to the essentials. "One way of almost not being there, short of dying," writes Lisa Heschong, "is to be deciduous, an adaptation displayed by plants not only in snowy climates but in desert climates as well." Broad leaves, just so much excess baggage when dropping temperatures lower the rate of photosynthesis, are retained only by species native to places where the winter is relatively benign or where there will be enough snow to cover them. Growth and the movement of sap slow almost to a stop. The rings on tree stumps are visible records of cycles of rapid spring growth bordered by winters of still-ness. Natural antifreeze may be accumulated in the form of fats or sugars in the cell's protoplasm, just as the bodies of some insects produce fat and glycerol, which enable them to survive extreme cold in a state of quiescence. Plants native to places with very low temperatures screen bacterial nuclei from their outer-most cells. Ice cannot form at the usual temperature without such nuclei, so water can remain a liquid to temperatures as low as minus 47 degrees C (–53°F). Some of the hardiest plants can even survive the inva-sion of ice between their cells.

A change in the weather is enough to renew the world and ourselves.
—Marcel Proust

This is not torture, at least not in midwinter, when hardy plants are able to endure temperatures far lower than they can in summer. In winter, these plants actually require a certain amount of cold. Their buds will not grow properly in spring if they are kept at room temperature all winter. Their seeds often need a period of chilling too, and so do hardy bulbs like tulips. These plants are not gluttons for punishment; the temperature has to fall to only about 7 degrees C (45°F) to satisfy them, but the ex-posure must be of a certain duration—from about 11 days to more than 40, depending upon the species—and it must be mostly unin-terrupted. Growers of hardy tree fruits are especially aware of their trees' requirement for an unbroken period of cold, which helps flower and leaf buds develop properly and encourages a bountiful crop. The type of tree an orchardist can grow is most clearly de-fined, in fact, by the winter—its lowest temperature and its con-stancy and length. The required cold period is shorter for peaches, longer for apples, but what is more surprising, a winter that stays very cold can be easier on trees than one that is not so cold and oc-casionally warms enough to encourage growth too early. When rock-hardy Siberian apricots that fruit on the prairies are grown in places where winters are warmer, they are apt to have their blos-soms killed by spring frost, one of many reasons for the myth of the nonfruiting "male" apricot or peach.

Frost on tender new growth is one of the most savage killers, wiping out peach blossoms on trees that easily survived much colder weather a month earlier and dispatching the swelling buds of forsythia, lilac, quince and willow alike. It is as though, with the warming days of spring, hardy perennials shed their mittens and, like children, cannot find them when they need them again.

57

Soft and vulnerable, the trees become like ourselves, unable to cope with much beyond the narrow range of comfort that lies snugly between the poles of fire and ice.

Baby Bloomers

Starting seeds indoors is one of my favourite spring rituals. There is something wonderful about watching tiny green stems growing toward a window when outside all is snow and ice. What I have is a garden in miniature: there are the peppers, there the tomatoes, there the onions, there the new cultivar of impatiens I have been wanting to try. Thirty or forty different plants may fill recycled polystyrene foam coffee cups, plastic pots and cardboard milk cartons.

For these indoor seedlings, temperature is a pressing matter. Room temperature, fortunately, is adequate for the germination of many seeds, especially the cold-tolerant vegetables long in cultivation, but many garden plants do better with higher temperatures, and some will not sprout at all without them. The good news is twofold: the high temperatures are necessary only until germination, and up to that point, most seeds do not require light. This means that flats or pots of moist potting soil and seeds can be moved to the warm places in the house where no one would presume to grow plants; on the refrigerator, perhaps, or beside the woodstove or on a furnace vent. The ideal average germination temperature is about 26 to 32 degrees C (79 to 90°F). Anything much hotter can bake the seeds, and they should be covered with a plastic sheet so that they do not dry out. Move the flats or pots into the light as soon as sprouts appear.

One year when I was germinating many heat-loving seeds, I turned the bathroom into a short-term greenhouse. The smallest heated room in the house, it also had a window for the few species that required light for germination. A small electric heater and a door kept closed between visits added up to a very high germination rate. Once the seeds had sprouted, seedlings were moved out of the bathroom and into other bright windows in cooler places, though no cooler than 15 degrees C (59°F), even at night.

Some seeds require a period of cold and dampness. Most flowers, shrubs and trees native to temperate places are like this. Grahame Ware, who sells the seeds of native British Columbia plants from his company Natural Legacy Seeds, has an easy scheme for the cold/wet germination process called stratification. He puts wet vermiculite mixed with seeds into a small plastic bag, labels the bag, rolls it up and stores it in the refrigerator at about 2 to 5 degrees C (36 to 41°F) for the required amount of time, usually two or three weeks. When the bags come out of the refrigerator, the seed/vermiculite mixture is pressed onto the surface of wet soil in a labelled pot, covered with a little more soil and placed in a bright, warm place—he uses a double 4-foot (1.2-metre) standard fluorescent fixture for lighting.

The seed companies that sell the type of seeds whose best germination temperatures are above or below the norm are also the ones most likely to tell you how to grow them. This information appears on packets and in catalogues such as those of Natural Legacy (RR 2 C-1 Laird, Armstrong, British Columbia V0E 1B0), Thompson & Morgan, Inc. (Box 1308, Jackson, New Jersey 08527-0308), Redwood City Seed Company (Box 361, Redwood City, California 94064; catalogue $1 to U.S., $2 [Cdn] to Canada) and Chiltern Seeds (Bortree Stile, Ulverston, Cumbria, England LA12 7PB; catalogue $4).

On Earth

The independent life of the soil became obvious to me one evening in late May when the vegetable garden had been spaded and the air was heavy with warm mist from a recent rain. When I entered the still mostly bare garden in the fading light, the scene before me resembled the seafloor more than anything terrestrial. The damp surface was writhing with earthworms that retracted with elastic swiftness into their burrows as I started to walk down a path. When I stood still, they emerged again, and all the soil's surface seemed to be in motion. Fascinated, I watched a dew worm about as long as my forearm fit its mouth around the fat white root of a sprouting broad bean and drag the bean toward its burrow. I felt a little like the owner of a restaurant discovering that as soon as I turned my back, the staff were dancing on the tables and eating the food from the customers' dishes.

I had never before witnessed the purposeful activity that went on in the garden when I was not in charge, although I knew only too well that if I stayed away from this bare soil for about a week, I would be greeted by a carpet of vegetation, evidence of the soil's own huge bank of seeds—more than 500 to a coffee cup of garden soil, according to Charles Darwin. Despite my calling this place mine, I had come to realize that I was a visitor. I had only a temporary influence upon a place with its own secret agenda.

Divine Earth, mother of men and of the blessed gods,
You nourish all, you give all, you bring all to fruition,
and you destroy all.
—The Orphic Hymns, *4th century*

The strangeness of the soil, its shyness and darkness, the way it makes plants appear and dead things disappear, the way it has a life of its own, has inspired people throughout the ages to feel everything from veneration to disgust. And why not be disgusted? Dirt is brown and looks suspiciously like excrement, and excrement, given air, water and warmth, eventually becomes dirt. In fact, everything once living can be reduced to this very common denominator, which will consume a fallen tree in a forest as easily as it will a fencepost holding up the garden gate. Dirt and filth are our terms for the most despised of everything, even people. Earth was one of the four elements of the alchemists, and bile was its expression in the human body. Gnomes are the legendary misshapen beings that inhabit the earth's hidden hollows. The ancient Japanese considered the earth the land of darkness or the land of roots, the kingdom of the dead where demons live.

On the other hand, earth has been respected as the source of life. It is easy enough to see that plants depend on the soil; pull one out by its roots and see what happens. Gardeners, too, depend on soil and are forever meddling with it. In past centuries, when a greater proportion of the population worked on the land, people believed that they also came from this brown matrix which had its own ability to create and destroy. According to Genesis, humanity came "from the dust of the ground." The first man, Adam, takes his name from the Hebrew word for earth, *adamah*. The word "human" comes from the same root as humus, as do humble, humiliate and the Persian word *zamin*, meaning land. In Greek mythology, Prometheus kneaded mud into statues that the goddess Athene brought to life. The ancient Babylonians, Egyptians and Chinese believed that the first human beings were made from clay, and in parts of Africa and North America, it was thought that the first people emerged from the earth.

If human beings were made from the dust of the ground, then earth would, in a sense, be mother, a word that comes from the same origin as matter and matrix. The ancient Chinese system that divides all things into yin, female, and yang, male, connects yin with the earth and yang with the sky. Confucianism, a Chinese religion with an authoritarian, logical orientation, is considered yang, whereas the nature-oriented Taoism is yin. ("Whoever is planted in the Tao will not be rooted up" is an earthy image in a poem by Lao-tzu, legendary founder of Taoism). Mother Earth, who at one time held dominion worldwide—called Pachamama in Peru, Asase Yaa by the Ashanti of Africa, Ceres by the Romans, Demeter by the ancient Greeks—is a personification of the ability of the earth to hold seeds, produce life and nurture living things. The words "fertile" and "barren" apply to both women and soil.

I find that a real gardener is not a man who cultivates flowers; he is a man who cultivates the soil. He is a creature who digs himself into the earth and leaves the sight of what is on it to us gaping good-for-nothings. He lives buried in the ground. He builds his monument in a heap of compost. If he came into the Garden of Eden, he would sniff excitedly and say: "Good Lord, what humus!"
—Karel Čapek, The Gardener's Year, 1931

This contrast of adjectives is inspired by that very thin matrix sandwiched between the unliving rock below and the unliving air above. Soil is largely a mixture of those two things, about half rock particles and one-quarter air. But sand, clay or silt alone is not soft enough to silence our footfalls on a woodland path, strong enough to keep huge trees upright or powerful enough to nourish them.

Soil is also about one-quarter water. It is a thick, gritty sea. Like the ocean, the soil sea is the home of living things that can exist nowhere else for long, and it is these peculiar creatures that turn rock, water and air into soil. Roots dry out in the air and may drown in water. They and almost all other soil dwellers will bake or freeze if exposed to above-ground temperatures year-round, but in the dark world underground, a temperate place that offers both air and water in the right manner and the right amounts, they thrive.

Roots must be treated carefully when they are transplanted, as must goldfish being moved from pond to pond. I like moving plants around even in midsummer—the worst time, everyone knows—and have found that I can move almost anything so long as I take a big enough root ball, move it immediately to the new place and water it deeply for a few days.

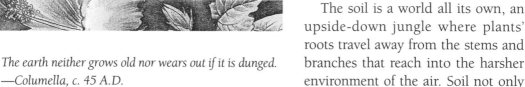

The earth neither grows old nor wears out if it is dunged.
—Columella, c. 45 A.D.

The soil is a world all its own, an upside-down jungle where plants' roots travel away from the stems and branches that reach into the harsher environment of the air. Soil not only absorbs warmth from the sun but also generates warmth. The air within it is different in composition from the atmosphere, and the water within it is different from that in lakes and oceans. The unique nature of soil makes it a brewing pot for minerals and other elements as they make their way from rocks to plants, from plants to animals, from animals to plants, from air and water to living things. The soil is a kind of go-between that breaks chemicals apart and builds new ones. In nature, it generates itself from the air, rain and sunlight, from all the living things that fall on it and from its own inner population of living and dying organisms.

Soil in nature is not like a hydroponic system. This sort of system, used a lot now to grow greenhouse tomatoes and lettuce, consists of an inert, homogeneous matrix, such as sand or vermiculite, that is dependent upon the energy of humans and machines for an almost constant supply of water and dissolved nutrients. In a greenhouse, even rainfall is excluded. Cut off the supply of nutrient solution for a day, and the plants may be damaged beyond repair. A garden is not like that, but seldom is it self-sustaining either, as is the ground in a woodland. A garden falls somewhere between those two extremes. The gardener who wants to maintain healthy plants must atone for his or her interference, and the best atonement treats the soil as a living system, not a hydroponic one. The soil works best when it is respected as the gardener's silent partner.

The earth has been compared with a human body, usually female, and with parts of her body—a breast or a womb—but a better metaphor is less romantic. Topsoil is most like a stomach. It accomplishes digestion for plants, most of which cannot do it for themselves. A 1950s government booklet about soil states this comparison in dramatic fashion: "Just as the food we eat is 'burned' (oxidized) in our bodies to provide us with materials for replacement of tissue and energy for our work, so organic matter is slowly 'burned' (oxidized) in the soil to provide replacement of humus and to give readily available nitrogen and minerals for the soil microbes and crop plants." The organic matter being burned, or digested, is made up of complex molecules—all kinds of dead creatures as well as the products of living things—that are broken down into simpler substances which plants can use.

The living creatures that do most of this digesting are tiny organisms, most of them as small as single cells; many others are larger but nevertheless visible only under a microscope. One gram (0.04 ounce) of soil may contain billions of bacteria, many metres of mycelia, which are threadlike

To you, grandmother, the Earth, do we offer tobacco also. We pray for victory in war and for all the medicines that are necessary to attain it, so that we may bind ourselves with medicine; that we may use the flowers of the earth for paint—all that is red and all that is blue—this we ask of you. Should there be anything better, we ask that you arrange it so that we obtain it. Tobacco and corn for food do we offer to you, and should you need more tobacco, we will send it along.
—Winnebago prayer

fungal cells, and about a million beings whose bodies are outerspace fantasies of legs and odd appendages. This huge population of the soil sea is busy respiring, eating one another, multiplying, growing, producing heat, absorbing water with its dissolved minerals, breaking molecules into atoms, gathering atoms into molecules, secreting and excreting various substances and then dying, becoming food for others. These creatures move through the water that laces the soil particles together. They do the work of the soil, and the gardener who feeds them is well on the way to feeding everything else.

Sir Edward John Russell, a British soil scientist with a tendency to philosophize, wrote in 1957: "A clod of earth, seemingly simple and lifeless, is now known to be highly complex in structure, its particles most elaborate in their composition, with numerous invisible crevices inhabited by prodigious numbers of living organisms inconceivably small, leading lives of which we can form only the haziest conception, yet somehow linked up with our lives in that they produce the food of plants which constitute our food and remove from the soil substances that would be harmful to us. It would be flattering to our self-esteem to think that they are there for [our] purpose, but it is safer to take the wider view and to suppose that they, like ourselves, are leading their own lives, the purpose of which is completely hidden from us."

It may be too anthropomorphic to assume that these microorganisms have any purpose of their own other than, perhaps, staying alive as long as possible—if they do, it certainly will remain their secret—but the purpose of some of them within the matrix in the soil is known. Some bacteria, for instance, are capable of taking nitrogen from the air and turning it into a form plants can use, a very rare and valuable ability; in French, nitrogen is called *azote*, without life, because almost nothing living can use it in its elemental form. Our own bodies breathe elemental nitrogen in and breathe it right back out again; we obtain nitrogen from our food. When certain soil bacteria work in partnership with the roots of legumes such as peas, beans, lupins, caraganas and a few other plants, they will do their work of adding nitrogen to the soil. Other soil dwellers are capable of breaking proteins into their precious building blocks of carbon, nitrogen, oxygen and other elements. Provide them with organic matter to digest, and they will work.

Speak to the earth, it shall teach thee.
—Job XII:8

All of what Russell calls "inconceivably small" organisms are affected by the gardener, by every turn of the spade and every application of fertilizer, water and compost. In a native woodland soil, almost all of them live within the top 5 centimetres (2 inches), but in the garden, they are flipped over and dug in deeper. Their populations rise and fall with the changes in the soil's air content, which come with our tilling, with the changes in its water content, which come with our irrigation, and with the changes in the amount of food they get, which come with our fertilization.

A much more visible example of the human influence on the soil is its population of earthworms. The most productive species of garden earthworms, such as red wigglers, manure worms and night crawlers, are not native to North America. A survey undertaken in Arkansas in 1961 revealed that of 17 species identified, only 6 were native. These underground inhabitants of plowed soil have accompanied the migrations of humanity like the seeds of weeds, and like those plants, earthworms are, at the root of it, healing and medicinal.

Aristotle called earthworms "the intestines of the earth," and they look the part. In fact, if one is what one eats, then earthworms are just so much soil in a different form. Unusual creatures entirely suited to the strange sea of earth, they are as streamlined as eels. Headless and deaf, they can sense light. They breathe through the skin and are very sensitive to touch, thus their quick response to my footfalls in the twilight garden. They are hermaphroditic— male at one end, female at the other. They mate end to end and, while doing so, may feel a wormy sort of bliss: "While copulating, the worms do not respond readily to external stimuli such as touch and light," write two scientists who have studied their quiet ways. Charles Darwin, a painstaking observer, wrote an entire book about earthworms, which he thought exhibited signs of intelligence because they always pulled objects into their burrows from the narrowest or pointed end.

Nor indeed can all soils bear all things. By riversides willows grow and alders in thick swamps, barren mountain ashes on rocky hills; on the seashore, myrtle thickets flourish best; and the god of the vine loves open slopes as yew trees do the freezing north.
—Virgil, Georgics II, 3rd century B.C.

Whether or not earthworms are intelligent, they are loved by intelligent gardeners for their bodies, not their minds. No matter how my plants do, I feel a rush of self-congratulatory pleasure whenever I pull aside the hay mulch and see a cluster of earthworms. In New Zealand, where European settlement and agriculture came later than in North America, soil scientists charted the rapid spread of introduced earthworms. As their population rose, the soil was able to support more lush growth of grass and richer forage crops, even without fertilizer.

Earthworms make the soil more porous by tunnelling, which is helpful for plant roots and all air-breathing soil dwellers, including the worms themselves. They carry soil from the surface downward, acting like slow, silent tillers, and they digest soil to produce castings, which are considered the finest humus: perfect topsoil that needs no additives. The nitrogen in their castings is in forms such as ammonia, urea and uric acid, which can be readily used by plants. Charles Darwin wrote: "It may be doubted whether there are many other animals which have played so important a part in the history of the world as have these lowly organized creatures."

When I was gardening editor of *Harrowsmith* magazine, I heard from several Alberta gardeners about the earthworm problem they were having. It seems the worms were turning their soil into a hard Swiss cheese of tunnelled clay. I received a holey baseball of a sample that had survived the journey in a cardboard box. The worried gardeners had tried everything from poisons to plowing. But nothing had worked, because the problem, of course, was not with the worms but the soil. The earthworms, immigrants like the gardeners themselves, were simply making the soil's problems obvious.

More organic matter—much more—would gradually turn the clay into topsoil. Getting rid of the worms would simply produce hard Emmenthaler without the tunnels.

The mud becomes rock-hard when it dries. It is so sticky that when you walk across the yard after a rain, you must keep moving, because once you quit, you are stuck. One year, we planted trees on the field. It was wet, and I stayed in one spot too long, and my boots would not move. I had to get out of them and plant the rest in my bare feet.
—Betty Schlichting, Sanford, Manitoba

I had silty clay soil in my last garden, not quite as bad as the Alberta clay, but it was heavy enough that if I worked it too early in the spring, I had a field of hard lumps all year. If I kicked one of those lumps, it broke into a pile of useless powder. When the soil was wet, it stuck to my spade, and when it was dry, it cracked under the summer sun. Clay soil is described as heavy because, in comparison with other types of soil, it really is. Its particles of rock are so fine that they hang onto each other and onto water, excluding air. Plant roots have trouble making their way into clay, and so do earthworms; the Alberta worms must be especially determined.

Not that clay is necessarily the worst soil a gardener can have. Sandy soil, which has the largest rock particles of all soil classifications, presents its own difficulties. Water and fertilizers slide right through it. When I was frustrated with my heavy clay soil, my next-door neighbour was frustrated with her sand. I scarcely watered all summer, but if Debbie didn't water every day, her garden wilted as though it had been tortured by a wind off the Sahara.

What we were both aiming for was similar. We both wanted soil that looked something like chocolate cake, and we wanted earthworms. Gardeners have probably always wanted that kind of soil, which explains the way they lust after manure piles, much to the incredulity of nongardening friends. More than 300 years ago, John Parkinson wrote: "No man will deny, but the natural black mould is not only the fattest and richest [soil], but far exceedeth any other, either natural or artificial, as well in goodness as durability." Debbie and I wanted the same thing, but we were starting from very different places. How could we make our way from here (clay and sand) to there (black mould, as Parkinson called it)?

What both of us needed was organic matter. It is living things and their detritus that turn sand or clay—or silt, whose rock-particle size falls between those of sand and clay—into loam. Loam is soil that contains a substantial amount of humus or organic matter or compost, different terms for what might be the same material. Loam feeds earthworms and other living things in the soil; they in turn can feed the plants. Loam is a kind of savings bank which holds water and fertilizers so that they are available to plants when they need them. Loam acts as insulation too, warming quickly in spring and staying warm in fall. A spade pushes easily into loam and so do a root and an earthworm.

One morning I went to the garden. I saw Lao Chou make a trench about 4 or 5 feet deep and it was close to the west wall. Then he dropped some offal into it; poured plenty of water over it; then he covered it with soil. I asked what it was for. He did not answer me but smiled gently. "Tell me, Lao Chou," said I, "what are you going to grow in the trench? It must be something very rare and precious. I guess you are planting Tibetan water lilies or Indian lotus, aren't you?" "I just want to grow something beautiful." —Su Hua Ling Chen, "Our Old Gardener," Country Life, February 16, 1951

Adding organic matter to soil simultaneously makes the soil better and fertilizes the plants. In nature, this happens as a matter of course. Dead vegetation falls on the ground to decay and return to the plant roots. But it does not necessarily happen in agriculture. I once visited some seed-growing companies in California whose fields had such poor, lumpy, compacted soil that the plants in it struggled along between absolutely essential waterings and feedings. None of the soil's organic matter had been replenished, so the fields had become close to hydroponic—unable to sustain themselves for long without human help. Gardeners can do better. On our smaller scale, we can easily make up for the deficit of organic matter we create every time we cart away the clippings left by the lawn mower and every fall when we rake the leaves and clean out the dead tomato plants and blackened asters.

Synthetic fertilizers can have their place. I use them indoors for houseplants and the seedlings I start. The amount I use is minuscule, and the balance of nutrients is correct, so I don't feel any remorse at this lapse from organic practice. But outdoors, I use only compost and mulch and occasionally some bone meal. My garden manages to stay as healthy as any others I see, and the soil looks better every year. I like knowing that I am working with the soil, not just the plants. It is not really possible to work with just the plants; the illusion that one can do so is a precarious business.

I am no soil scientist, and what looks like a nutrient deficiency to me, tempting me to reach for the fertilizer, could well be caused by a plant disease or by soil that is too warm or too cold, too wet or too dry, too acidic or too alkaline. I am not reassured by those pictures of perfect vegetables and perfect roses on fertilizer labels, because while soil scientists are able to figure out exactly what a hydroponic tomato needs in the way of minerals, they do not know what is already in my soil. Adding fertilizer might create more problems than it solves—a situation that is common in gardens as well as farm fields. What does reassure me is the advice of soil scientists who have no vested interest in selling boxes of packaged Tomato Food. A bulletin from the Ontario Ministry of Agriculture and Food states, "For the home gardener, the use of crop refuse supplemented by composted household wastes may be quite adequate for continued production of fruit and vegetables without the use of chemical fertilizers. In this case, the household wastes coming from an appreciable portion of purchased food add to the nutrients returned in crop refuse."

If gardeners will forget a little the phrase "watering the plants" and think of watering as a matter of "watering the earth" under the plants, keeping up its moisture content and gauging its need, the garden will get on very well.
—*Henry Beston,* Herbs and the Earth, *1935*

Of course, I am not growing only fruit and vegetables, but those are the most fertilizer-hungry things in my garden. The flowers need less feeding, and shade trees should be entirely self-reliant. If, as the Ontario bulletin states, the fruit and vegetable garden can be adequately supplied by kitchen garbage, then so can the entire garden.

What my garden receives in the way of organic matter is kitchen garbage and livestock manure, both of which are composted. Manure not only supplies organic matter but also effectively recycles nutrients, especially nitrogen, back to plants from animals. Even human urine is safe in a compost pile, though human feces are a risky fertilizer—they can carry the eggs of parasitic worms and the germs of diseases such as cholera and may be contaminated with heavy metals, the traces of our industrial life style. Composted sewage sludge, where available, is only for lawns and ornamentals.

Gardeners have made their way with organic matter for centuries, growing legumes for nitrogen and digging them in for good measure, but we can be a bit more scientific. A soil test can determine roughly what the soil contains; roughly, because the test measures only a tiny sample of soil. One thing the test will show is the soil's pH, the measure of its alkalinity or acidity.

I had a couple of soil tests done on that clay garden. One, done by the provincial ministry of agriculture, showed that the pH was 5.9, so my soil was acid. (Any number under 7 denotes acidic soil.) Another test, done by an independent laboratory that makes organic recommendations (Woods End Laboratory, RFD 1, Box 4050, Mount Vernon, Maine 04352), showed the same pH and recommended the application of 10 to 15 tons of manure per acre to increase the organic-matter content.

If a healthy soil is full of death, it is also full of life: worms, fungi, microorganisms of all kinds.... Given only the health of the soil, nothing that dies is dead for very long.
—*Wendell Berry,* The Unsettling of America, *1977*

Acidic soil—called sour because acids taste sour—is normal in a fairly cool, rainy climate like that of eastern Ontario. Liming with calcitic limestone (almost pure calcium carbonate) or dolomitic limestone (which contains about 20 percent magnesium carbonate) are the usual prescriptions for neutralizing acidic soils. Another possible treatment, lime, which is limestone heated to form calcium or magnesium oxide, is fast-acting but expensive and so caustic that it can burn plants. The garden where I work now is quite close to my previous garden, but this one has alkaline soil, with a pH of about 7.5, because its bedrock is limestone.

Gardens like mine or in other dry places usually have alkaline soils. They can be made more acidic with sulphur, pine needles and peat moss. Alkaline soils are called sweet, but alkaline substances taste not so much sweet as bland, like milk of magnesia. In solution, they feel slippery or soapy.

Knowing whether the soil or irrigation water is acidic or alkaline can explain some garden phenomena: why the hydrangeas are pink or blue (acid makes them blue); why the daisies thrive and the heathers die (daisies tolerate alkaline soil, heathers do not); why the potatoes are scabby (the soil is alkaline enough to allow scab to proliferate); why blueberries die (they need very acidic soil). Also, it explains some nutrient deficiencies in plants, because certain minerals are more available in acidic soil than in alkaline and vice versa, a complicated issue which means that farmers of certain crops adjust the soil pH to increase fertility. Knowing one's soil pH is not necessarily a reason for altering it, however. I never did add limestone to my previous garden, even though I discovered the soil was acidic. Such a change can be very helpful—most vegetables, for instance, do best in soil close to neutral, around pH 7—but soil modifications that use mined minerals should be done slowly and in moderation.

You ask me to plow the ground. Shall I take a knife and tear my mother's breast? Then when I die she will not take me to her bosom to rest. You ask me to dig for stone. Shall I dig under her skin for bones? Then when I die I cannot enter her body to be born again. You ask me to cut grass and make hay and sell it and be rich like white men. But how dare I cut off my mother's hair?
—*Chief Smohalla of the Nez Percé*

Drastic changes in the soil can be damaging, and once the soil is damaged, it is difficult to heal. It is the same with fertilizing. Too much of any additive is worse than too little. Almost all minerals or elements are supplied to the soil in the form of salts. Salts dissolve in water, which is the form in which plants use them, but in this form, any excess can wash into nearby waterways or be deposited on the soil surface as the water evaporates, leaving a white crust. The plants themselves can be harmed by too high a concentration of salts or by an alteration of the soil's own mineral supply.

Perhaps more to the point, the mining, manufacturing and shipping of these soil additives are harmful to the environment, something gardeners, of all people, should care about. Mineral deposits are finite, and their effect upon the soil is only temporary. This is true of any mineral additive, whether it is supposed to alter the acidity or alkalinity of the soil or provide nutrients, like a bag of Tomato Food, Rose Food or Lawn Food. Most nitrogen fertilizer comes from a process that requires large amounts of fossil fuels. Phosphates and potash must be mined. Something is askew when gardeners set out to create a beautiful environment around their own home while at the same time helping deplete natural resources and despoiling the environment elsewhere.

For most gardeners, the best road to a healthy garden is to select the plants that suit the existing garden soil and then work to improve it by adding compost, mulch and other organic additives. Plants that need soil different from the native soil should be confined to a single area where they can be treated together.

A test, as simple as making a mud pie, can give the gardener a new perspective on the soil. It is not as instructive as a laboratory soil test, yet it shows what is there and can be repeated all over the garden for no cost at all. Last summer, I filled a glass jar about half full of topsoil, covered the soil with water, then shook the mixture into mud. In one shake, I undid all the mixing the soil's earthworms and other living inhabitants had done. The sand sank to the bottom, and successively smaller rock particles settled in quite clearly defined layers above it. On top was the humus, with its bits of grass and roots. By repeating the test as often as I wanted, I could clearly see which parts of the garden were mostly sand, which were mostly clay and where there was the most organic matter. It helped me to see what was already there before I set out to meddle.

I think of the earth now as a sort of living thing—Mother Earth, or even Mother Earth's stomach—that needs to be nurtured. The grass is not always bright green. It might look more like a prairie than a lawn, but the soil is improving, the garden is lush enough, and I am not doing much harm to the world beyond the garden. Henry Beston writes in *Herbs and the Earth*, "No soil under heaven will suit everything unless it be that loam we vicariously left behind in the first of gardens: we have to do our best with what we find."

Top Soil

Turning soil that looks like a gravel road, a sand dune or a lump of modelling clay into something resembling chocolate cake can be a very slow process. Earthworms will help, but only if the soil is already in fairly decent condition. The answer for all soils is compost, fortunately a substance that is free for the making, even though it does take some time and demands raw materials. Compost improves soil not so much because it adds nutrients in large quantities—its analysis is, in fact, quite low—but because it improves soil structure and porosity, brings the pH closer to neutral and thus makes whatever nutrients are in the soil more available to plants. Richardson Wright was editor of *House and Garden* magazine when he observed in the 1920s: "No place is so small but it can afford an obscure corner for a compost heap; no gardener so busy but he can attend to its simple requirements."

My compost bin is three-sided, lidless, about 1.2 metres (4 feet) long and divided down the middle into two sections. One side is always filling. The other side is either being used or sitting for a few months until it is ready to use. My compost is made up mostly of livestock manure, kitchen wastes (no meat, which attracts dogs), garden clippings (no branches, which take too long to break down) and weeds (no twitch grass, which might take root). We do not rake the lawn, but if we did, the clippings could be forked in as well. Lawn clippings should not be left in a layer on the pile because they form an almost impenetrable thatch, and they should not be added at all if they come from a lawn that has been treated with herbicide. I do not layer ingredients but just throw them on as they become available, although I do cover the pile with a sprinkling of topsoil or finished compost from the other pile every so often to introduce soil microorganisms. I water the pile if it looks dry. It takes about six months of warm weather to make compost in my garden.

Leonato: Well, niece, I hope to see you one day fitted with a husband.
Beatrice: Not till God make men of some other metal than earth. Would it not grieve a woman to be over-mastered with a piece of valiant dust?
—William Shakespeare,
Much Ado About Nothing, c. 1598

Leaf compost is an excellent soil conditioner too, but it takes longer to make: about three years. Leaf compost is too low in nutrients to be considered a fertilizer—its nitrogen content, on a dry basis, may be less than 1 percent—but like any compost, it aids water absorption and soil aeration and helps to neutralize soil and so make minerals more available.

The composting procedure, which is very complex in its chemistry, is the essence of simplicity in practice. It involves heaping biodegradable things, preferably broken or chopped into small bits, in one spot until the pile is about half a metre (2 feet) high. An occasional turning with a pitchfork will bring the top and edge bits toward the middle. The pile must be fluffy enough and dry enough to allow oxygen to penetrate through it, but it must also be damp enough for the fungi and bacteria that do the work of decomposition to thrive. Microorganisms dead and alive make up about one-quarter of the weight of finished compost.

The bacteria and fungi in the pile require carbon for growth and nitrogen for protein synthesis. A higher proportion of carbon means slower composting; a higher proportion of nitrogen, faster composting but increasing loss of nitrogen into the air as ammonia. High-carbon compost ingredients, such as straw, paper and sawdust, are often relatively dry and brownish. They should be used only in very small amounts, if at all. High-nitrogen ingredients tend to be lush and green, like grass clippings and garden weeds, or they are animal by-products: manure, urine, blood meal.

Given air and dampness, the pile can become as hot as 76 degrees C (170°F). The chemical process that goes on in a working compost pile is aerobic decomposition, meaning "with air"; it is a very slow sort of combustion carried on by microorganisms. As in any fire, oxygen is consumed, heat is produced, and the finished product is darker and takes up a good deal less space than what was there at the beginning; compost typically reduces by 60 or 70 percent.

I add compost to the surface of garden beds every spring, and if I am making a new bed, I mix as much of it as I can into the soil. When I am growing plants in containers, I may use compost on its own or mix it with soil.

As if it were not enough that compost improves soil in almost every way, compost-making also means that less garbage and fewer plastic bags (full of leaves, garden clippings and kitchen garbage) are being trucked to landfill sites. Every garden store sells bins attractive and discreet enough for city gardens, while in the country, a simple homemade enclosure like my own is fine. Composting with earthworms is possible indoors. There are books that describe all these processes, as well as horticultural societies and departments of agriculture that will assist anyone interested in nurturing the earth with the earth's own produce.

On Stone

Very close to my garden is a natural stone sculpture both wonderful and rare: a meteorite crater. I can see it from the window of my office on the second floor of the house. Next to the house is a flat field and beyond that the tops of trees, then another field. The treetops mark the spot of a meeting between heaven and Earth that took place at least 500 million years ago, long before people or dinosaurs or even fish existed. Much later, an inland sea covered the area with limestone and turned a crater 244 metres (800 feet) deep into a gentle valley. Although this valley is not actually a part of my garden, it reminds me and all who stop to look at it of the power and presence of stone, which shapes the world and every celestial body to the end of the universe. Stone is the backbone of our gardens and ourselves.

There is no meteorite in the crater, but if there were, geologists say that it would be about the size of a 30-storey building—a substantial presence. People would come from far away to look at it. Not as pretty as gold, silver or diamonds, meteorites are still among the stones the world values most highly in a spiritual sense. The famous black stone set in the Kaaba, an ancient stone cube in the centre of the Moslem world's holiest place, the Great Mosque in Mecca, is a meteorite. Other meteorites have been praised as gifts from Zeus or symbols of Mother Earth.

Now slides the silent meteor on, and leaves
A shining furrow, as thy thoughts in me.
—Alfred, Lord Tennyson, "Now Sleeps the
Crimson Petal," 1847

Small meteorites hit the Earth quite frequently and are considered serendipitous prizes. Norman Lockyer writes about a couple that landed in England two centuries ago: "The two largest found, of 74 pounds and 48 pounds, fell by the roadside, and a lawsuit to settle whether they were the property of the finder as being wild game or of the owner of the lands adjacent as being real estate was decided in favour of the owner of the land."

Stone has its own rules concerning space and time. It seems to make certain otherwise invisible things, such as time and gravity, visible. The sands of time that slip through an hourglass are a particularly poignant symbol of the brevity of the human life span when compared with the relative permanence of stone. To the Maya, a stone, or *tun*, was a measure of time 360 days long. They also measured time in *katun*, spans of 20 years, in *baktun*, 400 years, in *pictun*, 8,000 years, in *calabtun*, 158,000 years, and in *kincultan*, about three million years. Poor weary Sisyphus of Greek mythology was punished by having to push a huge stone to the top of a hill, watch it roll to the bottom and push it up again—over and over through the *katun, baktun, pictun, calabtun* and *kincultan* that measure eternity.

Working with stone does tend to slow a person down, which suits the purpose of a garden but is a backbreaking frustration to farmers. Where I live is stone country. The nearest city, Kingston, has been nicknamed the Limestone City, in honour both of its many quarries and of its grey century-old stone buildings and garden walls. This glacier-scraped part of southern Ontario is also studded with erratics, boulders left after the last ice age. Surprisingly, an enormous globe of granite in a flat field is not the eyesore one might expect. Simultaneously calming and eye-catching, funny and graceful, a large erratic is a geological joke with a Magritte-ish sense of magic. When I drive past a big one, I always turn to look.

Regrettably, my family's garden has no erratics big enough to command attention, but it is full of stones left by retreating glaciers, from the little ones near the surface of the ground to the increasingly large ones I unearth as I dig farther down. They are all gifts from somewhere north of here and have been on this property for about 10,000 years, a wink of geological time. When I dig even deeper, I go back further in time until I hit the limestone that was here when the glaciers

Your skull can sit on someone's desk two hundred years from now, but it won't be you, it's just a mineral deposit, a tombstone. Bones as stones: you too can make a wall.
—John Jerome, Stone Work, *1989*

scraped the topsoil away. If I could drill much deeper, I would reach the granite that was on the surface when our meteorite hit half a billion years ago. The limestone bedrock is not very far under the surface of the soil, sometimes only as deep as my trowel, and sometimes bedrock shoulders erupt above the ground: bones of the Earth, as the Japanese put it. Bedrock is the tip of the Colossus that holds up the garden and connects it to the centre of the Earth.

Stone is visible in gardens in outcroppings of bedrock and in smaller rocks, in gravel and in sand. Stone creates the contours of the garden and determines whether gardeners must cope with hills or valleys or level ground. Less obviously, stone shows up in concrete, metal, glass, terra cotta, pottery and brick, even in vermiculite and perlite.

The sand, silt and clay in the soil are actually finely pulverized rock. The work of water and living things will make that rock's minerals available to plants and ourselves. Take the organic things away from the sand, silt or clay, and the result is a desert—the sands of time—waiting to become garden again. The indigenous people in what is now southern Manitoba considered an expanse of sand a holy place, because sand was one of the first elements of creation, closer to the great spirit than any living thing.

Certainly, rock was here long before we were. The calcium, phosphorus and magnesium that make human bones and teeth strong came originally from stone. The same elements are needed for the work of plant cells, but the strength of plants—and plastics, for that matter—comes from carbon and its organic molecules, such as cellulose. Carbon, which comes not from stone but from air, is strong —diamonds, the hardest objects known, are almost pure carbon— but, atom for atom, carbon is lighter than oxygen. It is the featherweight among body builders; stone is the heavyweight.

I am a rock, I am an island,
And a rock feels no pain,
And an island never cries.
—Paul Simon, 1965

A chunk of limestone about as big as two fists—too small to be much use in the garden and far punier than the flagstones I have tipped into reclining wheelbarrows— weighs something close to the British measure of weight called a stone, 6.3 kilograms (14 pounds). It is a substantial presence in my hand and soon strains the muscles in my arm. People who work with big stones need ropes, pulleys, pry bars, draft animals and cranes. The Japanese love large uncarved stones in their gardens, some of them as big as the erratics in farm fields around here. Stones as tall as people can weigh 25,000 kilograms (25 tons), about as much as five full-grown Asian elephants. In describing how to move large stones without expensive machinery, the book *Japanese Stone Gardens* cautions that a large falling stone is not a friendly thing. For instance, "when a stone is significantly taller than wide or has a protruding base, the wire rope is liable to slip dangerously off."

Lafcadio Hearn, an English journalist who went to Japan more than a century ago, married a native woman and became a Japanese citizen, was very impressed by all things Japanese, including the use of stone in the landscape. He wrote in 1904: "You cannot walk through a street without observing tasks and problems in the aesthetics of stones for you to master. At the approaches to temples, by the side of roads, before holy groves and in all parks and pleasure-grounds, as well as in all cemeteries, you will notice large, irregular, flat slabs of natural rock—mostly from the river beds and water-worn—sculpted with ideographs, but unhewn. These have been set up as votive tablets, as commemorative monuments, as tombstones and are much more costly than the ordinary cut-stone....Again you will see before most of the shrines, nay, even in the grounds of nearly all large homesteads, great irregular blocks of granite or other hard rock, worn by the action of torrents and converted into water-basins (*chodzubachi*) by cutting a circular hole in the top."

These design principles were taken to their extreme in the Zen Buddhist dry garden—which, lacking large plants, might not be considered a garden at all, just a design in stone with its accompanying moss or lichen. Large, craggy stones, each one carefully selected for size and shape, are meticulously and firmly positioned within a sea of pebbles raked into parallel lines. The garden is not meant to be entered, only to be viewed. From outside, the viewer looks inward and meditates upon a design that may suggest islands in the sea or the Buddha surrounded by his disciples.

This isn't the kind of garden I want for myself. It is very foreign, in every sense of the word, to my ideal, which is a place of chaotic abundance, but I do love to see a beautifully designed dry garden. I saw one first thing one morning, and as the early yellow light shone into it, I watched a man with a saw-toothed wooden rake precisely arrange its pebbles into a design of parallel waves. Every so often, he stopped and moved one or two misplaced stones with his fingers. The slow raking itself seemed a kind of meditation and was a pleasure to watch. The design of the garden and even the action of the man with the rake suited the silent, unmoving presence of the large stones.

Constant dripping hollows out a stone.
—Lucretius, 99-55 B.C.

Another term for such a garden is "dry lake." In the Japanese landscaping tradition, there are also dry rivers and dry waterfalls. In all of them, stone alone suggests the waterscape. The dry river is a path of stones that follows a riverlike course, wide or narrow, through the garden. It is not meant for human traffic—its stones may be neither flat nor particularly secure. It follows a contour of land where water might realistically flow. As such, it may need to be excavated so that it will lie between higher banks. The rocks should appear as though positioned and weathered by running water. The effect can be lovely and, without requiring the troublesome and expensive installation of pumps and pipelines, can be surprisingly evocative of the sound, sight and soothing effect of running water where none exists. In some Japanese gardens, the dry river is formalized, with currents of raked sand that seem to swirl and flow between larger rocks. A dry waterfall is a series of tumbling crags down a steep slope. A bridge can span any of these features to connect one bank with the other.

Isao Yoshikawa, the head of the Japanese Garden Research Society, advises in *Japanese Stone Gardens*: "Arranging stones well takes years of patient practice. It is not something that can be easily explained in words or understood by seeking the advice of someone else or found even in the so-called secret books of centuries past."

81

Years of patient practice are likely to pay off with stone, thanks to the simple fact that it normally stays where it is stacked. Some ancient monuments and sacred places are very impressive in size and longevity. The largest Egyptian pyramid is still mammoth 40 centuries after the mountain was built from limestone building blocks weighing as much as 45,000 kilograms (44 tons) apiece. Stonehenge, western Europe's largest prehistoric monument, is a circle of sandstone bridges balanced on uprights more than 6 metres (20 feet) high.

Unless you can feel, and keenly feel, that stones have character, that stones have tones and values, the whole artistic meaning of a Japanese garden cannot be revealed to you.
—*Lafcadio Hearn,* Glimpses of Unfamiliar Japan, *1894*

It is a testament to the cultural significance of both the Great Pyramid at Giza and Stonehenge that they were made from stones brought from far away: the construction site was as important as the material itself. Scientists in the intervening centuries have gone to a great deal of trouble to figure out how many people, along with rafts, pulleys, draft animals and wooden rollers, were needed to move those gigantic stones—more than 32 kilometres (20 miles) in the case of Stonehenge. In a recent reenactment of the creation of Stonehenge, a dozen men were able to drag one 1,800-kilogram (2-ton) bluestone on wooden rollers, with another dozen picking up the rollers from behind and running to the front to replace them. At least 180 people, it was estimated, would have been needed to raise one of the 23,000-kilogram (23-ton) uprights into place. Three thousand years later, they are still there.

I was lucky to visit Stonehenge in the 1960s when it had not yet been fenced. Anyone could park by the highway and wander freely through it. In fact, one huge stone had been decorated with a painted peace sign, the upside-down Y designed in a time when nuclear war seemed imminent. In that silent, sacred place where the midsummer sun still rises directly over a central stone, the sign, circular in its own right, seemed not a defacement but a plea.

It was a reminder, too, that decorating stone has to be done with care. Not many messages—or colours, for that matter—are appropriate upon a canvas that is so powerful. Pictographs done by indigenous people are wonderful, but painted stones in the garden seem like attempts to slap clown makeup on the faces of ancient philosophers. The effect is quite different from that of painted wood.

Stone is most beautiful when it shows its own colours, evidence of its long history and the minerals it holds, and it is never more imposing than when it appears as a mountaintop above the treeline. There, the backbone of the Earth touches the sky and seems to pierce heaven. Clouds circle the peak, snow and ice last all summer, and lightning flashes nearby; the four ancient elements of earth, air, fire and water are united at the craggy summit. Until this century, the highest peaks were beyond the physical reach of mortal humanity, so mountains were deemed gods themselves —or the homes of gods. Mauna Kea, Fujiyama, Kilimanjaro and Everest have all

*The Master…lets himself be shaped by the Tao,
as rugged and common as a stone.*
—Tao Te Ching, c. 500 B.C.

been considered deities by the people who lived on their flanks. Seat of the Greek gods was the misty top of Mount Olympus, which rises dramatically from the shores of the Aegean. In North America, the Pueblo people believed that their four sacred mountains were pillars that held up the sky and divided the world into quarters, while the Apaches believed that mountains were not only alive but also the source of the shaman's power. The Mextecs, a Mexican tribe, buried their dead in a cave high on a mountain that they believed was a gateway to paradise.

However small a piece of stone in the garden may be, it carries some of this power and dignity. Of course, stone is only relatively permanent, and even the people who revered mountains knew well that stone was a changeable substance. When I first hiked in the Rocky Mountains, I was surprised to see that the summits of the mountains, which looked solid from a distance, were cracked and crumbling. Everywhere I looked was evidence of the modifying effects of ice, wind and gravity. Below the summits were aprons of scree, stones that had tumbled from the tops. The paths toward the mountains passed through meadows that consisted of a thin skin of topsoil over beds of this fallen rock. The mountains were on their way to becoming hills, then plains. Highly magnified photos of eroding rock show something that resembles rotting fruit more than anything eternal. Stone is made of the same minerals we are and is vulnerable, too, to ageing. It is long-lasting only in comparison with living things. Its changes are either slow or dramatic.

Stone can be damaged by water, air, plants and changes in temperature. It can be broken, melted, dissolved, scraped and compressed. J.E. Gordon reports that when a person stands on a brick laid on its side, the brick is compressed one fifty-thousandths of an inch, "an inconceivably small distance but a perfectly real movement for all that." Stone staircases used for centuries are transformed into series of hills. Any bare cliff shows the tortuous history of that bit of the Earth's crust. The stone has been pressed, pushed, bent and fractured. It has melted and solidified. It may have moved from a seafloor to a mountaintop. It has gradually weakened with the temperature changes that inevitably come with day and night and the progression of the seasons. Water courses over its surface, carrying particles away. Water also seeps into cracks and then freezes in cold weather, expanding and breaking the surface. Rainfall takes in carbon dioxide from the air to form a weak acid that eats rock.

Lichens, often the first living colonists of rock, also break it down. Lichens are the perfect match for rock. They, too, are hard, slow to change and likely to outlive us. They survive farther south and north than any other plants. Lichens that form crusts on rock increase their dominion of the world at no greater a rate than one millimetre (0.04 inch) a year. Some are 40 centuries old.

Lichens are unique marriages between fungi and algae. The alga in the partnership carries on photosynthesis, while the fungus secretes acids that dissolve the underlying rock and release its minerals. Lichens eventually produce a tiny bit of soil, an environment hospitable to mosses, which in turn create enough soil for small flowering plants. Increasingly large plants have ever stronger roots that open cracks in the rocks, breaking them further. By examining lichen growth, scientists can estimate the age of ancient stone sculptures and can tell how long a patch of ground has been bare since the last ice age. Incredibly tough, able to withstand drought, freezing and baking, lichens are nevertheless also among the first plants to be damaged by air pollution because they have no means of excreting any of the harmful elements they absorb.

I met a traveller from an antique land
Who said: "Two vast and trunkless legs of stone
Stand in the desert. Near them, on the sand,
Half sunk, a shattered visage lies, whose frown,
And wrinkled lip, and sneer of cold command,
Tell that its sculptor well those passions read
Which yet survive, stamped on these lifeless things,
The hand that mocked them, and the heart that fed:
And on the pedestal these words appear:
"My name is Ozymandias, king of kings:
Look on my works, ye Mighty, and despair!"
Nothing beside remains. Round the decay
Of that colossal wreck, boundless and bare,
The lone and level sands stretch far away.
—Percy Bysshe Shelley, "Ozymandias," 1818

84

Stone, too, is vulnerable to pollution. City rainfall that is dilute sulphuric and nitric acid challenges sculptors and chemists trying to protect statues, gravestones and buildings. (These people use the word stone only to describe rock that has been transformed by human hands; rock is the natural substance. I am using the terms interchangeably.) Outdoor structures built centuries ago that have remained almost pristine have been transformed swiftly within the last couple of generations into mounds of what looks like melted wax. Saints and soldiers alike have lost noses and ears, angels have become hills, gargoyles are lumps. The same thing, of course, is going on in our gardens, on our rock walls and birdbaths and paving stones, but we are not so apt to see the effect in our lifetime. Were we to notice it, we would realize that even where the garden's stone is concerned, the garden is a place of continuous change. The final step in the erosion of rock is its incorporation into the earth as particles of sand, silt or clay.

The changeability of stone, which makes it much like living things, made sense to the people of past centuries who thought of stone as truly living. As recently as the 17th century in Europe, minerals were thought to grow in the manner of plants, and pebbles were assumed to be young rocks. Crystals will, of course, precipitate out of saturated solutions of certain minerals; they will grow even though they are not alive. According to mediaeval alchemists, however, metals had a life of their own. Over the ages, lead would turn to copper, copper to iron, iron to tin, tin to mercury, mercury to silver and, finally, silver to gold. This theoretical chain of events could be speeded up if one could find the elusive philosopher's stone, which would not only turn metals into gold, so they said, but might also heal the body and the spirit. According to legend, this stone may have been lost by Deucalion, the Greek Noah figure who recreated humankind after the deluge by throwing stones over his shoulder. His stones became men; his wife's, women.

The gardeners of China and Japan take into consideration the changeability of rock when they situate it in their gardens. Since an Oriental garden is considered to take at least 300 years to mature, gradual alterations that occur in its elements are anticipated and enjoyed. The colonization of stone by lichens, then mosses, adds greatly to its appeal. The Chinese were the first people to deliberately incorporate natural uncarved stone into garden designs around the fourth century A.D., encouraged by their interest in

Buddhism, with its focus on meditation. The aim was to create miniature mountains and rugged landscapes whose beauty people could appreciate without having to go on a long journey.

In the West, the rock garden is a much more recent development. It was never envisaged as a showcase for rocks but as a habitat

for certain plants. Purists choose only true mountain natives; the challenge is that many alpine plants are not only difficult to obtain but are difficult to grow beyond the mountains. It is relatively easy to give them the excellent drainage and stony soils they demand but impossible to duplicate most other characteristics of high meadows: a short growing season, extremes of temperature, thin air and relatively untempered sunlight. G.F. Scott Elliott writes of alpine native plants: "A queer point is that they have got so accustomed to this stormy and perilous existence that it is extremely difficult to grow them in a garden. Like mountaineers, they dwindle and pine away in the richer soil and softer air of the low grounds." Grahame Ware, who sells the plants and seeds of his mountainous region of British Columbia, confirms that gardeners sometimes give these plants such rich earth that they waste away for lack of gravel and sand.

If a stone can be lifted easily, it is inconsequential, and fetching it is a small but tedious chore. If lifting it gives me pause, makes me figure out ahead of time where I'm going with it when I get it lifted, the task stops being tedious. If the stone is more than I can lift, it becomes a project, requiring pry bars, rollers, the technology of moving heavy things—sports equipment for the game, the point of which is getting the most stone for the least effort. Big stones are more fun, making me try to figure out the physics.

—*John Jerome,* Stone Work, *1989*

Some places are gifted with natural rock gardens. Bedrock that shows through the garden soil can be one of the most beautiful garden elements, and it breaks neither back nor budget. The gardener who does not consider such stone a godsend—formal rose gardens and flat acreages of vegetables must be left aside for now—would be wise to think in terms of raised beds, containers, pockets of soil and ground covers such as thyme, sweet woodruff (*Galium odoratum*), creeping phlox (*Phlox stolonifera*) and, in the shallowest soil, *Sedum brevifolium*. Outcroppings and naturally occurring stones can give a garden an individuality and beauty that other gardeners would (and do) spend fortunes to emulate.

As if my garden does not have enough, my family has also taken to collecting stones and bringing them home. In this, we are far from unique. When Alexander Pope was not writing epic poetry or essays or translating the *Iliad* and *Odyssey*, he was placing stones in his English garden: "Lyttleton sent red spar from lead mines, Spence, pieces of lava from Mount Vesuvius...Mr. Cambridge, large pieces of gold cliff, Brazilian and Egyptian pebbles and blood stones, petrified wood and moss, fossils and snake stones, gold ore from Peruvian mines, crystals from the Hartz mountains, silver ore from Mexico, coral, copper ore, spar from Germany and Norway, curious stones from the West Indies."

Years ago, I used collected stones for edging beds, but I have since learned better. Keeping the weeds and lawn grasses out of the spaces between and around the stones was difficult, and mowing next to them was impossible. But within the beds themselves, surrounded by soil, stones of various shapes and sizes act as visual punctuation marks, as stepping places and as shade makers for plant roots.

Bringing foreign stone into the garden is a way of playing with the future. Once, at my former house, we found a stone hand axe buried deep in the soil, deep enough to suggest that it had been there for hundreds of years. In a *pictun* or a *calabtun* or a *kincultan*, will a geologist find one of my souvenir chunks of rock here, far from its home, and wonder how it arrived? By then, the crater will be an even gentler valley, but the discerning eye will still make out its contours, and the foreign stones hidden underground near its rim will suggest, perhaps, that here, long ago, was a garden.

Light Stone

Stone is not an easy material to shape. It is heavy and hard. Other materials made from minerals, however, are much easier to work with. They can be shaped or moulded when wet and, when dry, offer at least some of stone's hardness and attractiveness. Good-quality clay can be worked and then baked to make pottery. Concrete, which is a mixture of limestone or lime, sand and sometimes gravel, needs only water, not heating, and will harden as it dries.

One concrete mixture has been made especially lightweight by the inclusion of a 20th-century mineral ingredient, vermiculite, a mica compound heated so much that it has expanded and become porous. Vermiculite is commonly used as insulation and in seedling mixtures, in both cases because of its pockets of air. Perlite, another substance made from heated, expanded volcanic rock, can be substituted for vermiculite in the recipe below, as can builder's sand, which of course will make the mixture heavier.

I made outdoor planters one summer using lightweight concrete. In a shady spot, I spread out some sheets of newspaper. On them,

I placed my mould, an overturned 30-centimetre-tall (12-inch) plastic nursery pot, and covered it with a plastic bag, using string to help hold the plastic tight (elastic bands or masking tape will also work). Over this, I fitted a layer of chicken wire, which I removed and set aside until later.

Rock of ages, cleft for me,
Let me hide myself in thee.
—Augustus Toplady, 1776

The recipe for the concrete, which came from the newsletter of the Brooklyn Botanical Garden, was developed by H. Lincoln Foster and Laura Louise Foster. It calls for six parts vermiculite, four parts Portland cement and six parts well-crumbled, dry peat moss, which further lightens the mixture and gives it a rough appearance. I used a 1-litre (5-cup) plastic bowl as a measure, and the 16-scoop mixture was enough to cover one plastic pot.

I combined the dry materials, then stirred cool water into them until, as the Fosters describe, the mixture had "the consistency of sloppy cottage cheese. It should not be so wet that it is runny and impossible to shape with your hands." I pressed the wet mixture over the plastic until it was about 1.25 centimetres (0.5 inch) deep, placed the chicken wire on top, then added enough concrete mixture to cover the wire completely. The reinforced concrete should be about 2.5 centimetres (1 inch) thick on the sides and 5 centimetres (2 inches) thick on top. I smoothed the surface and inserted a couple of iris stems—dowels can be used—into the pot base (now the top) to make drainage holes and left the pot outdoors in a shady place to cure. After a day, it was somewhat dry, and I carved a design into it, then covered it loosely with a wet sheet to ensure that curing continued slowly enough to create strong concrete. In a couple of days, when the outside felt firm, I removed the stems, overturned the concrete pot, removed the plastic pot from inside and peeled out the plastic liner. I left the pot right side up, uncovered, for about a month before using it because plants can be harmed by fresh concrete.

Rectangular containers that resemble old stone troughs and sinks can be made with the same recipe. A cardboard box lined with

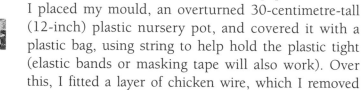

plastic can serve as a mould. Press the cement mixture on the inside of the bottom and sides, then add a layer of chicken wire to strengthen it and, finally, more of the mixture to cover the wire. Tear the box off when the concrete is firm.

Vita Sackville-West calls the trough garden "one of the handiest and most intimate forms of horticulture." When set up on bricks or stones, it can support very small plants that are best seen up close, and it can be enjoyed, with no bending necessary, she points out, by "the rheumatic or the sufferers from lumbago or the merely rather stiff-jointed elderly."

On Water

No wonder I like to sit under a tree on a hot day. Not only is it shady there, but the air is less dry: tree breath. In an hour on a summer day, a tall maple transpires about as much water as a hot tub holds. That's a lot of water to spread around in an hour, but not a drop is ever seen by someone lazing under the tree's branches as the water travels from earth through plant to air. Like the water in the maple, all the garden's water is on the move, and most of it is hidden from us.

It is hidden in the air, in the soil and in countless puddles that do not look like puddles but take on a fascinating, colourful multitude of unpuddlelike shapes—tree shapes, earthworm shapes, gardener shapes, tomato shapes, whatever—that hold the water, in transit, by means of relatively small amounts of substances other than water. A fresh leaf is about 80 percent water. So is a human being. An earthworm may be 85 percent water. A carrot or a strawberry is about 90 percent water, roughly the same as a mud puddle. The water content of a ripe tomato may be more than 94 percent. All of us are squishy and steamy, leaky and sloshy. Pierce us, and we drip; crush us, and we weep. Leave us high and dry long enough, and we wither, parch and finally die.

The rain cometh down, and the snow from heaven, and returneth not thither, but watereth the earth, and maketh it bring forth and bud.
—Isaiah 55:10

Some of the garden's water, of course, is not hidden. It shows up in real puddles and in rain, sleet, ice and snow. There may be watering cans to collect it and sprinklers to disperse it. There may be barrels under the eaves troughs and buckets of that beneficent homemade fertilizer, manure tea, steeping, ripening for use. Water may be employed as a landscaping device, in the form of a pond or a stream. When water shows its face in these deliberate water features, we can take time to watch it and appreciate it.

"A pool is the eye of the garden in whose candid depths is mirrored its advancing grace," writes Louise Beebe Wilder. And our advancing grace too, she might have added. Still water is reflective, and it encourages reflection. Moving water, such as a stream or a fountain, is as captivating to watch as falling snow, and its sound muffles less pleasing noises. Japanese landscape designer Ken Nakajima says, "Because rainfall is an important element in Japanese scenery, water plays a great role in the landscaping of a Japanese garden. Water is very useful in depicting nature. It can be stored in ponds, released in streams and dropped as in a waterfall. Natural beauty can be expressed by the wind making ripples on the sunlit surface of the water; streams can be enjoyed as the water changes and takes on various forms." Just as in traditional Egyptian, Indian and Persian gardens, a central fountain or pond offered reassurance of survival in the desert or the wilderness, fountains in modern cities are visual and audible oases.

Water itself is a remarkable substance. It is a liquid, of course, and although that may not at first seem remarkable—every solid and gas becomes liquid at a certain pressure and temperature—in truth, we are familiar with few liquids other than water; water, that is, in its many guises, from milk to sap. We are unfamiliar, though, with pure water, something rare and ephemeral. Pure water is like the beautiful Undine of myth, the elemental spirit of water, according to Paracelsus in the 16th century. Undine was created without a soul, but if she bore a child, she would obtain one and, by extension, all the suffering that comes with mortality. In Friedrich La Motte-Fouque's story, Undine says to her mortal husband, "One of us can only win a soul by the most intimate union in love with one of your race." Water, too, takes on the power of life by its association with life. Water is like a biblical translation of the mystical name Yahweh: "I am what I am becoming."

Water is a good servant, but it is a cruel master.
—*John Bullein, 1562*

And water becomes an astonishing variety of things. It can be a food or a poison, an acid or a base. The rain that falls on my garden is as acidic as tomato juice because as it falls, it mixes with sulphur and nitrogen oxides released into the air by cars and industry and thereby becomes dilute sulphuric and nitric acid. Water molecules can insinuate themselves into the molecular structure of most other matter, so water is a very effective solvent, capable of dissolving sugars, amino acids and many salts. It carries minerals into plant roots and nutrients into our own bodies.

Water is both strong and flexible. Its strength—the surface tension that allows flat rocks to skip over a calm lake—also allows evaporation from leaves to pull it hundreds of feet skyward to the tops of trees and vines. The surface tension arises from water's tendency to bind to itself. But it also binds to many other surfaces, which is why things become wet when water touches them.

Like all liquids, water changes shape easily. Pour it into a container, and it assumes the shape of the container: a watering can, a tomato, a cucumber, an earthworm, a gardener. Heat water, and it becomes a gas—steam, a haze, a fog, a cloud. Freeze it, and it becomes solid, and another set of structural possibilities arises. Most liquids become denser as they solidify, but ice floats in water. On a pond, this self-made lid enables living things, from fish to water lily tubers, to survive in any water remaining at the bottom. If ice sank, these living things would die. More to the point, they would never have existed at all.

The temperatures and pressures within which water remains liquid are pretty much the boundaries of life. Liquid water has been

93

part of every link of the unbroken chain of life since its birth, millions of years ago, in the water, which screened out the destructive ultraviolet light and acted as a sort of primordial spa, a kindly bath. A relatively large amount of heat is required to warm water; it also loses heat slowly. Swimmers are familiar with the phenomenon of finding lake water warmer than the air early on a summer morning but cooler than the air in the afternoon. The slowly changing temperature of the water affects the air too, thus coastal gardens enjoy a milder climate than inland ones at the same latitude and altitude. Bodies of water nearby greatly extend the northern boundary of plants, from magnolias and tea roses to kiwis and peaches. Large bodies of water have a greater protective effect than smaller ones, but even a garden pond will modify the climate ever so slightly and may help protect the plants in and around it.

The use of the bath, natural or artificial, has existed, in all probability, from the beginning of the world, since it is founded in the most natural wants of man.
—Chambers Information for the People, *1874*

But that is only one side of the aquatic story. All living things depend upon water, yet most terrestrial beings can drown in too much. Most plants extend their roots just into the water table, like children reluctant to wet anything above their toes. The first symptom of drowning roots, wilting, is a cruel and misleading one that tempts novices to water even more. Overwatering is a risk mostly with houseplants, whose excess water cannot flow away. Foliage hangs, turns yellow and drops as the roots rot. A drowning root is a bit like Tantalus of Greek mythology, who is parched with thirst although he stands in a pool up to his chin. The thirst, in the case of roots, is for oxygen, and they cannot use the overabundance of water. They can also die of drought if the water is too salty. "Water, water everywhere, / Nor any drop to drink," cried the ancient mariner of Samuel Taylor Coleridge's epic poem when his ship was becalmed in the ocean.

A narrow bridge connects water's power to destroy with its power to create life; that bridge is water's ability to cleanse and renew. Rivers overflow their banks, sweeping away everything in their paths, drowning plants and animals, destroying homes and uprooting trees. Yet when the floods recede, they reveal land that is refreshed and more fertile. Floodplains like the Nile's have always depended upon this annual renewal. This healing property of water is celebrated every time we have a bath and every time the rain cleans the dust off plant foliage, beautifying and allowing more light through.

On a much larger scale, a flood said to have covered the Earth and drowned all living things, save for a few chosen humans and other creatures—the Noah story—is repeated, in slightly different versions, almost worldwide. Only in Africa are such tales relatively rare. Whether or not these pervasive flood stories recall a real cataclysm, they do illustrate the power of water to transform and to destroy the past, a property ritualized by all religions. In many cultures, initiates are changed by passage through water, as were the Hebrews, who travelled trium-

Because water is transparent, it can receive light; and so it is fitting that it should be used in baptism, inasmuch as it is the sacrament of faith.
—St. Thomas Aquinas, 1225-1274

phant and unscathed through the Red Sea, blessed by God, and as Christians are baptized. The sacred Ganges River, said to flow from the toe of the god Vishnu, is where Hindus wash in order to be purified and where they scatter the ashes of their dead to be carried to new life. The Japanese, on their way to the tea ceremony, wash their hands in the fresh water running into a stone pond. The ancient Greeks believed that a taste of the water from the river Lethe, which flowed through the fields of the afterlife, washed away memories of former lives.

It is water's movement that does these things. All of the liquid in the garden, hidden or apparent, is always on the move, like rivers that appear and disappear, now visible, now secret, flowing out of our pores, out of the stomata of plants, out to the sap buckets, in through the roots, in through the lemonade, the whisky, the tomato, out through the lungs and the bladder. According to a Taoist metaphor, water is the blood of the world, while rock is its bone, earth its muscle, grass its skin and other vegetation its hair. What the followers of that Chinese religion were expressing, whether or not they understood it in detail, is that water has its own circulation system and in that respect is like blood. Water evaporates into the air and falls as precipitation, a cycle completed about 32 times a year. Water, then, remains in the air for just over a week on average. It is soon earthbound and, once here, spends a while in oceans, lakes, underground aquifers, rivers, sap, blood, sweat and tears until the heat of the sun pulls it heavenward again. Every living thing depends upon this endless movement.

The distribution of vegetation over the earth's surface is determined mainly by the presence of liquid water. Where rainfall is abundant all year, native growth is lush, as in a rainforest. Where summer droughts are severe and common, grasslands predominate. Drought year-round produces a desert with only lichens, perhaps, or

cacti. Gardeners, whatever their climate, tend to want lush gardens—we want the generous abundance of the rainforest even if we live in a desert, and we want greenery from spring through fall even if summers are dry—so a simulation of plentiful rainfall throughout the growing season becomes a pressing necessity and a duty relieved only by rain.

Until I lived near a spring in the country for several years, I did not know that water could have a taste. Only upon returning to the city did I perceive the insufferable difference.
—*Ginette Paris,* Pagan Meditations, *1986*

The constant movement of water may well turn the gardener into a terrestrial version of the astrological figure Aquarius, consigned to dump water from a vessel forever. I almost lost the first fruit trees I planted, because they looked sturdy enough, and I didn't realize that with their inadequate, damaged root systems, they required watering about once a week. In a study at the University of California, newly planted trees and shrubs watered deeply every five or six days produced almost five times as much top growth as plants watered half as frequently. The soil is a wonderful water bank—the top 100 centimetres (39 inches) of good loamy topsoil holds about 25 centimetres (10 inches) in storage—but plants can obtain only about half of that, and the weather seldom keeps the soil bank topped up. Usually it is too dry.

Too little water is the single most important factor limiting the growth of crops. Gardeners have, over the centuries, developed many ways of dealing with the life-threatening situation that arises when plant roots can no longer extract soil water. We have taken to dancing and singing, to praying, to swinging bull roarers, rattling pebbles in dry gourds and drumming on oak doors to mimic the sound of woodpeckers, once believed to be calling for rain. Now we rely on wells and pipes and sprinklers and trickle-irrigation systems on automatic timers that allow us a certain freedom, like mothers with wet nurses.

Fortunately, mature trees usually take care of themselves by tapping into underground aquifers. But shallow-rooted plants with big, delicate leaves are good at turning the gardener into Aquarius, especially if they are planted in containers or on sandy soils, which hold as little as one-sixth as much water as clay and one-eighth as much as humus. Lettuce practically disappears when it wilts, a graphic if pathetic illustration of the structural value of water in a plant that consists of little else. Seedlings, too, and newly established plant-ings and plants in pots are almost as de-pendent upon the milk of human kind-ness as newborn babies. A collection of window boxes, containers and hanging baskets demands a gardener who is home every day of the week simply for water-ing, preferably twice a day. One reason for the mutiny on the *Bounty* is said to have been Captain Bligh's insistence that the ship's precious supply of fresh water go to its cargo of potted breadfruit trees rather than to the crew.

This application of water on drooping leaves seems to have the same stimulating effect as a little brandy on a man who is sleepy after wine.
—W.H. Davies, My Garden, 1933

A stripling breadfruit tree requires about as much water to sur-vive as a large person. Plants need an astonishing amount of water, about 17 times as much as people, weight for weight. This figure comes from the early-18th-century work of Stephen Hales, who compared the water requirements of people with those of sunflow-ers. The human body circulates its water supply, so in a temperate climate, we need to take in only 1 to 3 litres (or quarts) of water a day to replace what is lost in urine, sweat and breath. But almost all of the water taken in by plant roots is lost from the leaves.

So roots, especially young roots—which do most of the plant's drinking—have a pressing job. It is so critically important that in the warm seasons, roots grow incessantly and in extravagant num-bers. Apple roots grow as much as 27 centimetres (10 inches) a month, while the roots of corn, a plant which must grow from seed to human height and produce a crop of fat, fleshy seeds within a few weeks, may grow 52 to 63 millimetres (2 to 2.5 inches) a day. This soon gives a plant access to a lot of soil in a fairly small area. A mature plant of crested wheat grass was found to have more than 500,000 metres (310 miles) of roots in about 2.5 cubic metres (88 cubic feet) of soil. That includes literally billions of root hairs, the smallest and youngest cell-thick extensions of roots, which are able to penetrate the tiniest spaces between particles of soil.

In a plant's circulation system, a cold tea made up of water and dissolved mineral salts moves upward in the inner part of the stem through a system of overlapping vessels called the xylem. In certain trees, the xylem traces a spiral pattern. The degree of spiralling can change from year to year and can even reverse direction. In dogwoods, the xylem spirals almost 90 percent of the way around the trunk with every metre (3.3 feet) of ascent. The final destination of this dizzy journey is the canopy of leaves, with their pores—stomata—that allow almost all of the water to escape during respiration. "Unfortunately," writes Paul Kramer in *Water Relations of Plants*, "a leaf structure favourable for entrance of carbon dioxide is also favourable for loss of water."

The downward vessel system, on the outer side of the xylem, is the phloem, whose fluid is comparatively syrupy. It moves much more slowly than that in the xylem and stops being produced when photosynthesis shuts down after sunset. The day's last feed of sucrose creeps downward at the rate of about a metre (3.3 feet) an hour, so it might not reach a tree's roots till morning. Aphids tap into phloem because they are after sugar, and they take in so much that they excrete the excess as a sticky honeydew beloved by ants. Desert-dwelling cicadas (*Diceroprocta apache*), on the other hand, tap into xylem, because what they want is water. They ingest so much that they actually drip and so manage to stay cool at temperatures of 43 to 46 degrees C (110° to 115° F).

Here again is water on the move. These cicadas routinely lose 20 to 30 percent of their body water every hour. "To put this into perspective," writes Eric Toolson, who studied the insects in the Sonoran Desert of Mexico, "humans die if they lose more than 7 to 10 percent of their body water, and most insects cannot tolerate losses of more than 15 to 20 percent." Clearly, the desert trees tapped by cicadas are under added water stress, but desert plants are such efficient water conservers that they can survive much drought abuse. They have strategies like closing their stomata by day and opening them at night (most plants do the opposite) and losing their leaves after the rainy season. On average, they take almost twice as long to dry out as drought-susceptible species. A few cacti can lose 70 percent of their stored water and survive, a feat bettered only by certain earthworms and lichens.

Cacti and their fleshy kin the succulents have stems or leaves that visibly balloon with water after a rain and gradually shrink as the supply is used. These plants, such as Christmas cacti and the jade plant (*Crassula argentea*), are almost ideal for negligent gardeners.

If crust-forming lichens were more interesting to us than the "pet rocks" marketed a decade ago, they might be even more ideal. The species that inhabit the deserts of the Arctic can endure years of drought by becoming so dry that they are only 2 percent water—about the same as many seeds. When rain does fall, they can quickly absorb as much as 35 times their weight in water and can resume photosynthesis.

Many waters cannot quench love; neither can the floods drown it.
—Song of Solomon 8:7

Seeds survive drought in much the same way—and not just seeds of the plants that await rain on the desert but also seeds of the countless temperate natives that await spring. Winter, in places where all surface water turns to ice, is, after all, a season of drought for plants. Their roots cannot tap into ice. Many trees and other perennials prepare for winter by losing leaves, profligate dispensers of the water that will soon be in short supply. They are jettisoned in favour of a sleek new watertight profile. Next year's infant leaves, formed during summer, are tightly swaddled by scales that keep water inside the way a rain jacket keeps it out. Evergreens have leaves so well suited to water conservation—needle-slender and waxy—that they can be retained throughout the winter to continue carrying on photosynthesis while losing little moisture.

The only environments in which water conservation is not a concern are places where there is always water, such as rainforests, ponds and riverbanks. Plants may be totally immersed—some of these are prized for their ability to bubble oxygen into garden ponds—or they may want only their roots in water. For humanity, the most important of the submersible-root plants is rice. The most sacred is another edible plant, the lotus (*Nelumbo* spp), which confidently links the realms of earth, water and heaven. Its roots are in the bottom of the pond, while its big leaves and beautiful, fragrant flowers are held in the air. "On rainy days, especially, the lotus plants are worth observing," wrote Lafcadio Hearn in *Glimpses of Unfamiliar Japan*. "Their great cup-shaped leaves, swaying high above the pond, catch the rain and hold it a while; but always after the water in the leaf reaches a certain level, the stem bends and empties the leaf with a loud plash and then straightens again." The lotus is such a singular plant that it was revered by early Egyptians and is still honoured by Moslems, Buddhists and Hindus.

Symbolic of the divine nature of humanity that rises from the mud of creation, spirit rooted in the flesh, the lotus plant itself offers perfect evidence of the ability of water to move from one thing to another, settling in ponds, filling cells, splashing from leaves. Only about one-fifth of the lotus plant is anything other than water, and we humans are much the same—filled, fed and sustained by the same fluid: *eau de vie*, the water of life.

Age of Aquarius

Somewhere there may be a garden that is self-sufficient in water, but it is not mine. Most of the gardens I know must be watered in some places some of the time; some must be watered almost everywhere almost all of the time during the growing season. And anyone who has houseplants knows the tug of the umbilical cord that holds gardener to garden year-round.

Because my own tap water, which comes from a well, is cold and very hard, I collect rainwater for my houseplants. Our tap water is alkaline and full of mineral salts. If I use it on houseplants, it eventually leaves a pale crust on pots and the soil surface and can interfere with the work of the roots. Houseplants prefer slightly acidic, softer water. Rainwater is the perfect solution, not only for myself but for anyone whose tap water contains substances that can harm plants over time. The fluoride added to city water, for instance, helps reduce tooth decay in children, but as little as ¼ part per million—less than most communities add—can harm many species of plants, such as freesias, gladioli and Easter lilies. Symptoms of fluoride poisoning can range from burnt leaf tips or margins to leaf death. Chlorine, too, can harm plants. Chlorinated water should be allowed to sit for about a day so that most of the gas dissipates. That will also allow the water to reach room temperature, which is ideal for houseplants.

Collecting rainwater is simply a matter of placing a container under any dripping spout from the roof. I bring a bucketful indoors and store it in the basement. A smaller bottle is always upstairs warming to room temperature before I use it on my plants. Only in January and February am I likely to run out of my rainwater supply and have to turn on the tap.

I use rainwater for my outdoor garden too, as much as possible. Two clean oil drums sit under the downspouts from the roof. Only about an hour's steady rain will fill them, and once full, the pair will take me through a week of daily watering, which I do by walking around with a couple of watering cans. Because my method is so minimalist, I cannot water everything all the time but have to be selective about the most needy plants. I never water the lawn, but then I don't mind if it fades for a few weeks at the end of summer. Newly planted things get most of my attention. I sometimes make manure tea by adding a bucketful of manure to one of the barrels and irrigating with the water that collects on top.

I have no system yet to collect grey water—the water that comes from washing—but in the places where it is legal, grey water can be used in the garden with a few restrictions. It should not contain borax, softeners or bleach. It should not be used on edible plants, on newly planted seedlings or acid-loving species, as it is apt to be alkaline. It can be used on the lawn or perhaps the perennial border. Using grey water is recommended in xeriscaping—landscaping for dry environments, specifically for the dry-hot of prairies and deserts rather than the dry-cold of the Arctic. Xeriscaping is a term coined by the hard-pressed water department in Denver, Colorado, in 1981, when the city's landscapes accounted for 40 percent of water use. Expensively treated and transported tap water can be used where it is most needed if rainwater and grey water, free for the taking, are gathered by the gardener.

On Paths

I cannot think about garden paths without thinking about life journeys. They are simply too similar, too muddled up together to separate. A path is something I can walk on or dream about. Dream gardens and real gardens are not so very different, after all. They become expressions of one another. Only the gardener knows where one ends and the other begins: where sleep ends and waking begins. Sometimes even the gardener doesn't know. The path extends out from the dream, illuminated by moonlight, and the gardener walks into the sun.

But let me describe two paths—two real paths—that might be considered opposites. To reach the first, which is in Massachusetts,

I walk along a trampled line in a lawn to an opening at the edge of a woods straight ahead. In the woods, the path is easy to follow. Enough footsteps have passed along it that there is no vegetation on it, as there is on either side. When I go up a hill, the path is either simply sloped or made into rough stairs with roots or stones. It is a narrow path, just wide enough for one person, and it passes through the kind of forest I can see a long way into because there is not much underbrush. The path follows the contours of the land as though it has been made by wild animals or livestock. It takes me through the woods for about an hour and finally comes out the other side to a country road where one seldom sees either cars or people.

O see not ye yon narrow road,
So thick beset wi' thorns and briars?
That is the path of righteousness,
Though after it but few enquires.
—Anonymous ballad,
"Thomas Rhymer"

The second path is near Beijing, China, at the Summer Palace. A century ago, the empress, who was accustomed to almost unimaginable luxury, used to retreat here from the steamy city, bringing along her retinue of hundreds of eunuchs and maidservants. Paved with a mosaic of patterned tiles, this path skirts a placid pond the colour of jade, full of lotuses, water lilies and orange carp. The path, which is wide enough for me and my husband to travel side by side, goes over several bridges and passes under arches bearing intricate paintings of birds and flowers. Crowds of other people are here too, Chinese people who seem familiar with the place as well as tourists with cameras. The path takes us around to a pavilion with benches overlooking the lake; finally, it leads us to the place where we started: the path's end is its beginning.

Both of these paths are real, and although they are very different, both could just as easily be symbolic of passages on the human journey through life. The first path I described might represent the narrow and rugged path of the solitary journey, and the second, the wide, smooth path one travels in the company of others. Those are the metaphors of the religious life, from the straight and narrow path of the Christian to the *shariah*, or path, that is Muslim law, to the middle way of the Buddhist. Yet there are other ways in which these paths seem like pictures out of dreams. The first path is poverty, where my feet will get muddy in the rain and dusty in dry weather; the other is the path of riches, where my every footfall will be met by a hard, even surface as intricately decorated as a carpet. The first is a path of wilderness and discovery, the second a path of history. The first takes me from one place to another; the second takes me back to where I started. But in each case, something is learned along the way: both paths make the journey as important as the destination.

That is not true of all paths. When I moved to the farmhouse that is now home, I encountered yet a third type of path. Leading from the gravel driveway to my front door, this path was a perfectly aligned row of perfectly square concrete slabs that ran parallel to the house wall and then made a precise right angle to turn toward the door. It was all too good an example of a purely functional path, more like a sidewalk, really, one whose creator has assumed that reaching a goal is the only reason a path exists.

It took me 10 years to learn that a woods is a wilderness until there is a path through it, for a path provides a point of view, a place from which the best features of the woods can be enjoyed.
—*Jeff Cox, 1993*

Like any path, this completely functional one did have its positive aspects. It provided reassurance that people had been this way before, that I was being led somewhere worth going in a way which would guarantee me at least a measure of safety. The main attraction of any path, after all, is its promise that I will not get lost. For ancient Egyptians travelling on the desert, where losing one's way could mean losing one's life, the fertility god Min was protector of travellers and guardian of roads. On the desert, a straight path was a blessed thing. In the seemingly straight path of the sun across the sky, the Egyptians saw the symbol of their own life journey, and the sun's reappearance every morning was a sign that they too might enjoy an afterlife.

A goal-oriented path is often straight, without a hint of nonsense. It is the arrow that points toward the bull's eye. Wealthy and powerful people have been able to provide an instant vista of the extent of their property by running a road straight from the front door to the boundary. Trees are cut down and hills levelled to make such engineering possible.

The straight path declares the human mastery of nature, and so it has its precedents in some very grand roads and *allées*, like the one that leads to the palace at Versailles. Any irregularity in the king's road might have hinted at unsteadiness of rule—and what could be a straighter symbol than that? The Romans were great at making straight roads at home and as far away as their conquering armies advanced, but the tradition is far older still. A Stone Age processional road 98 kilometres (61 miles) long with parallel earthen banks in Dorset, England, required more than a million days of human labour to make. Straight but crumbling roads still lead to temples and pyramids thousands of years old. In a very small way, the straight path to my front door—now replaced—suggested, too, that at least for these few steps along life's journey, I had better move right along rather than wander a few steps to smell the roses.

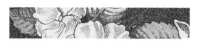

The path into the light seems dark,
The path forward seems to go back,
The direct path seems long...
—Tao Te Ching, *c. 500 B.C.*

This is not to say that even in a garden, a straight path or an essentially functional path is necessarily a bad thing. Between the rectangular beds in the all-white garden at Sissinghurst are straight paths paved with chevrons of brick that superimpose the purpose-fulness of daytime's clear vision upon the ghostly shades and shapes of twilight. Rosemary Verey's *potager*, or kitchen garden, in Gloucester is a delightful design of concentric squares and crisscrossing paths between beds of dill, lettuce and other herbs and vegetables. I welcome straight paths where wheelbarrows have to go or where there will be irrigation or simply where the main thing I want to do is avoid stepping on the plants, as in a vegetable garden. In a herb garden, the traditional geometric pattern of paths, straight or curved, makes sense, not only because it brings visual and spatial orderliness and makes shoots and leaves easy to pick but also because it suggests that the owner has mastery of the plants. I find it comforting to think that the gardener can tell the wormwood (*Artemisia absinthium*) from the tarragon (*Artemisia dracunculus*). A geometric herb garden may be enough to fool me until dinner.

In an ornamental garden, geometric paths suit beds of plants that are the same height and often the same colour, like marigolds or petunias—not my idea of great beauty but a good way to brighten public gardens, where maintenance needs to be kept to a minimum and straight paths are a practical way to move people around, espe-cially if they are in wheelchairs or strollers. The straight path suits the formality of plants that are under strict control, like rows of pot-ted oranges, topiary yews and roses on standards, clipped like poo-dles' tails. In the early 1700s, when these things were in fashion, an English gardener said he wanted his trees to stand in a file "Im-prov'd by Discipline, like a martial Band."

At a time when people believed that all of nature would make perfectly logical sense as soon as they could figure out God's neat plan of longitude, latitude, globes, orbits, days, years and other measurable things, the meandering path of dreams had little place in the groomed landscape. "Universallie walks are straight," declared William Lawson in 1619, in his book *A New Orchard and Garden*. Within a decade, Galileo Galilei presaged Isaac Newton by writing that the universe could be understood only if an observer "first learns to comprehend the language in which it is written. It is written in the language of mathematics, and its characters are triangles, circles and other geometric figures."

A different idea of the language of the universe can be seen in the dramatic use of winding pathways in a native American ceremony. "As most of the 'temples' the world over, the Big House of the Delaware Indians— a tribe belonging to the Algonquian stock—symbolizes the universe," anthropologist Margot Astrov writes, using the 1931 journals of Frank Speck. "The White Path is the hard-trodden dancing path outlined on the floor of the Big House, winding from the east door down toward the north, passing around the two sacred fires and again around the centre post, upon which the image of the highest manitou is carved, doubling back to the south and from there to the west door, the exit, the place of sunset where all things end. The White Path is the symbol of the transit of life; it stands for the road of life down which man wends his way with iron inevitability. But it also stands, according to Frank Speck, for the journey of the soul after death, for it corresponds to the Milky Way, the path of souls."

For the Side Grounds, you are to fill them with a variety of Alleys, private, to give a full shade, some of them, wheresoever the Sun be. You are to frame some of them, likewise for shelter, that when the wind blows sharp, you may walk as in a Gallery. And those Alleys must be likewise hedged at both Ends, to keep out the Wind, and these closer Alleys must be ever finely Gravelled, and no grass, because of going wet.
—Francis Bacon, Of Gardens, *1625*

The irregular path which suggests that the journey is as important as the goal has been carefully developed in the Oriental landscaping tradition born in China and adopted and altered in Japan. In both of these countries, garden paths are envisioned from the start, not popped in where there happens to be an open space after the planting has been done. The material may be plain or as ornate as a mosaic of coloured stones or chips of tile or brick. *Yüan Yeh*, a 17th-century Chinese gardening text, directs: "One should pave the paths with stones not larger than pomegranate seeds; they will then become beautiful and durable. Some use stones as large as goose eggs to produce the patterns, but such patterns are not long lasting

107

and tend to produce a vulgar effect....In between the stones one may use roofing tiles with which to form patterns."

The central importance of the path within the garden makes sense in cultures influenced by Buddhism, a religion that repeatedly uses the metaphor of the path. The devotional life—the road that avoids all extremes—is described as the middle way. This metaphor, no more complicated than the Christian straight and narrow, is, however, made more complex by the Buddhists, who also describe the religious life as the threefold path of holiness. The three expressions of the middle way consist of morality, meditation and wisdom. And this three-faceted road is described in greater detail as the noble eightfold path, whose eight aspects are right understanding, right thought, right speech, right bodily action, right livelihood, right moral effort, right mindfulness and right concentration. This path of correctness governs every moment of life, every breath, thought and movement. But the path is quite possible to follow, Buddhism teaches, if the traveller pays attention to all eight aspects. Each one makes the others fall into line.

Depart not from the path which fate has you assigned.
—Message in a fortune cookie

The classical Japanese garden might be the best example of the Buddhist doctrine made manifest. Here, the path is an aid to meditation: right concentration and right mindfulness. The older Shinto tradition, too, which teaches that various outstanding natural objects such as stones and trees are possessed of spirits, has had an influence on the Japanese garden path. It is most important that the garden visitor slow down and take notice of these carefully chosen and situated objects.

When I first stepped into the Japanese garden at the Montreal Botanical Garden, I already knew a bit about its designer, Ken Nakajima. I had talked with Pierre Bourque, director of the Botanical Garden, who had explained that Nakajima is considered one of Japan's living treasures, one of a select group of people who are retained by the emperor because their skills are so valuable. Bourque had watched Nakajima spend hours positioning each huge stone in the garden in just the right place.

Nakajima's path is designed to reveal the beauties of various aspects of the garden while simultaneously suggesting the sensual offerings of nature as a whole. The path suggests the place of the traveller within both the real and the spiritual worlds. Unlike the Chinese garden next door, which is a bustling, noisy place, the Japanese garden in Montreal can be fully appreciated only when it is fairly quiet in the morning or during bad weather. At such times, I could not help but notice certain things: that crossing a wooden bridge brought different sounds and sensations than walking on gravel; that a huge chunk of green stone was positioned so that it dwarfed the traveller on one corner; that the rush of a waterfall was visible and audible from one spot on the path, but both sound and sight of water were screened entirely by a dip of the path behind a grassy hill. The paths were all curved, which is traditional, not only to encourage the visitor to slow down and take notice but also because good spirits are thought to be attracted to a sinuous path, while bad spirits can pursue someone on a straight path.

The principle of a sufficient reason should never be lost sight of in laying out walks…that is, no deviation from a straight line should ever appear for which a reason is not given in the position of the ground, trees or other accompanying objects.
—*John C. Loudon,* Encyclopedia of Gardening, 1822

There is more than one way around this garden. It has places where the traveller can make choices. So what happens when a single path, straight or wandering, becomes two paths, or three paths or four? If you are inclined to believe in spirits, you might hope that the bad spirit behind you will take a wrong turn and leave you alone. The crossroads is a very special place in mythology, in dreams, in religions and, by extension, in all landscaping traditions. I do not feel that I am pursued by spirits, but still, at every fork in the path, I find there is both tension and freedom. I am led no longer; now, I must make a choice. In a garden, the reality of the choice is probably without risk: in Nakajima's garden, do I want to continue around in the wider outer circle, or do I want to go down a few steps to cross the small wooden bridge over the pond? But in my imagination, a fork in the road is never benign. Every choice can be good or bad, right or wrong.

In the metaphorical sense of the life journey, one's entire future depends on the decision made at every intersection along the way. The Hollywood car-chase scene, with its quick turns, holds my attention because of its familiarity. All of us know, if only from our nightmares, the feeling of panic when someone is behind us in hot pursuit and we must make the right decisions quickly. Crossroads are also places where we are more likely to meet up with other people. Greetings and departures happen there, and again, our lives are changed forever. In mythology, crossroads have often been associated with gods, demons, fairies and ghosts. Witches' gatherings were thought to take place at crossroads, which were also places to find cures for certain mysterious ailments such as the evil eye.

The deer, foxes and brush wolves have created paths that I use to enter or to leave the wood at its southern reaches. These trails are useful to the dogs but can be treacherous to an upright human being, since they are made by beasts whose shape and stature have little or nothing in common with mine.
—Timothy Findley, 1993

For one African tribe, the Bambara, a two-pronged fork in the road signifies doubt, but the four-branched crossroads is a very different thing. It represents the moment of creation. This is not at all an unusual idea. The centre of the crossroads is a powerful place where opposing forces are united, like the warp and weft in weaving or even the "crossing" of plants and animals. For native American people, the four-branched crossroads signified the four compass points, the four seasons, the four winds and four colours, often red, yellow, blue and white. Jesus Christ is at the centre of the Christian cross, and for centuries, all cathedrals had floor plans designed in the shape of the cross. At the centre of the ancient foursquare gardens of Persia, which mirrored Persian descriptions of paradise, was a well or fountain, symbolic of the water of life, or a tree, the tree of life. In any garden, an intersection or a place around which a path circles calls out for special treatment.

A bridge is a type of pathway and a type of crossroads. Bridges need not cover water. Some of the most artfully designed gardens elevate a path over a shady flowerbed or simply a span of gravel that mimics a dry lake or river. The simplest bridge is a plank or a flat rock, but bridges can also be very fancy affairs. In an Ontario garden, I once reluctantly crossed a wooden one shaped like an inverted U. It looked pretty from a distance, like something from Venice, but turned out, upon closer acquaintance, to be so steep that I had to take the weight off my skidding shoes by doing a hand-over-hand climb up and down the handrails. Needless to say, the bridge didn't add anything to the pleasure of walking through the garden. More than any other place on the path, a bridge must be absolutely strong and secure.

Whatever it crosses, a bridge gives the traveller the feeling of being above it all. That greater elevation, both real and metaphorical, offers a new perspective of the garden. But the path under the bridge is a different matter. While a position on a well-built bridge is one of safety and physical superiority in the sunlight, the shadowy place under the bridge is correspondingly inferior and even quite dangerous—the traveller can be hit, unseen, from overhead. Under the bridge, too, mischievous or even malevolent creatures may hide, like the trolls, one-eyed Scandinavian monsters. The place under a bridge is for me one of great discomfort. It is a place of nightmares. Only when I am travelling on water will I briefly and of necessity tolerate the dark experience of moving under the bridge, under somebody else's path.

When my garden was laid out, the paths appeared too wide, but as changing them would have meant expense and delay, they were not altered. Now, all along at the foot of the stone border verges are mats and tufts and trails of grey and green leafage—dwarf plants that have self-sown from the border above into the path, thriving there amazingly and creating the most delightful associations of colour and form, while they narrow my paths to more pleasing dimensions.
—*Louise Beebe Wilder,* Colour in My Garden, *1918*

It is worth remembering, when designing a path, that it will speak in many ways to the many people who travel upon it. In terms of the life journey, the path in the garden is an especially important one, because it means the last steps on the journey home and the first steps on the journey away from home. Step out of the house and onto the bricks, the stones, the gravel, the concrete. Step between the lawn and the junipers, between the herbs and the perennials, between one bank of snow and another bank of snow, and look ahead.

The garden path leads outward to the driveway or the sidewalk, which leads to a road, which leads to a highway, which leads, eventually, to larger highways and in turn to all the other highways on the continent and even beyond the continent, because highways lead to airports and ocean ports. The newly developing science of fractal geometry deals, in part, with this kind of connection. Just as twigs are connected to limbs and branches and capillaries are connected to blood vessels and arteries, so can you, as you go outward, take paths that become larger and larger, busier and more populated. The path may start with paving stones the size of pomegranate seeds, but finally, it is as large as the sea and the air.

Go inward, however, and each division can lead to a smaller

division with less traffic and ultimately to the individual path, perhaps the garden path, the way to the hearth and the heart.

Path Maker

I recently constructed a new path, my first such effort. About 9 metres (30 feet) long, it connects the front porch with the gravel driveway, replacing the path of rectangular concrete patio slabs that lay not much more than an arm's length from the house. This sort of concrete-slab path was frequently used around farmhouses like ours a couple of generations ago. It had the virtues of being cheap, sturdy and very easy to install—you just laid the slabs in a line on the levelled ground—but it offered nothing of visual or textural interest and was too close to the house to give me much room for gardening.

The new path, made of flattish pieces of limestone in various shades of grey, curves out from the front door and turns toward the driveway, widening as it goes, allowing a full 2.5 metres (8 feet) of flowerbed at its farthest point from the house wall. I chose the stones first of all because I love their appearance and sturdiness but also because this is the native rock of the area and so is piled around the edges of nearby farm fields, free for the taking.

The new path was easy to install because, like its predecessor, it has no foundation. I knew that a foundation of gravel might prevent frost from heaving the stones, but the gravel would have to be held in place behind an edging and would require an excavation about 30 centimetres (1 foot) deep. Close to the driveway, the limestone bedrock was almost at the surface. In any case, I didn't want a formal path with concrete between the stones. I had heard that it was quite possible to simply dig slab-sized holes out of the sod, insert each stone in place and leave the remaining grass growing between. If the stones heaved in the winter, they could be settled back into place in spring. During the summer, I could mow over the path. The neighbouring flower border could come right up to the stones because there would be no edging to worry about. Friends who had made paths that way were happy with theirs. The method seemed too easy to be true, but their pathways were beautiful and sturdy and easy to maintain.

I first marked out the position of the path with stakes and string. For a couple of weeks, as I walked to and from the porch in this newly defined area, I adjusted the stakes till the curve and width seemed just right. Then my husband John and I went rock gathering in his truck, looking for flat pieces of limestone that were thick enough to withstand footsteps without breaking and small enough for the two of us to lift together. Back home, we arranged the stones several times. We walked over the new path at each stage and discovered that we were happiest when there was a line of larger stones down the centre of the path, like stepping-stones, edged with some of the smaller ones. The outermost stones all had a fairly straight outer edge to give the path a clear border.

The path remained this way all winter, with the stones sitting on the grass. By spring, the grass under each stone was brown, a shadow image that I easily dug away with a trowel and a spade. As I inserted and levelled the stones in the turf and the new path progressed, I removed the old concrete slabs, then spaded the empty ground left behind, piled it up with compost and planted bulbs and perennials.

The new path, with the wider bed beside it, gives a very different feel to the approach to the house and to the surrounding garden. It is, I think, a thing of beauty in itself, and it makes its surroundings more beautiful by association.

On Walls

When Mary Lennox, heroine of Frances Hodgson Burnett's novel *The Secret Garden*, first hears of a walled, locked garden where she lives, she wonders, "How could a garden be shut up? You could always walk into a garden." It is an amazing discovery, to be sure—and such a powerful metaphor that the novel has remained in print for almost a century—but not because "you can always walk into a garden." All of our gardens are private property. They may not be walled or locked like the secret garden, but they are not to be freely entered.

There is a secret aspect to any garden, and this presents a moral dilemma to many gardeners. Garden walls can be beautiful things, and boundaries are necessary, but both circumscribe our desires to have our gardens resemble the natural world. Even more important, they get in the way of our cherished ideas about freedom. "Don't fence me in," croons the country and western singer, and we know exactly what he means. Our own boundaries protect us, but other people's boundaries restrict us. These inescapable facts, expressed by Janus, the Roman god of gates and doors who has two faces, can be difficult to handle in what is supposed to be a peaceful, welcoming thing, a garden. The words offence and defence, good military terms, both come from the same root as the word fence, the Latin *fendere*. So does fencing, the art of sword fighting. The inside of a garden wall or fence offers shelter and support, the unique habitat that brings order to tangles of honeysuckle, roses and clematis. But the outside is a barrier. Naturalist Margaret More Nice said of territory: "It is based primarily on a positive reaction to a particular place and a negative reaction to other individuals."

And thou, O wall, O sweet, O lovely wall,
That stand'st between her father's ground and mine!
Thou wall, O wall, O sweet and lovely wall,
Show me thy chink, to blink through with mine eyne!
—William Shakespeare, A Midsummer Night's Dream, *c. 1594*

Many of the most beautiful stone walls now crumbling around European gardens are reminders of times when the walls had a greater purpose than simply supporting the ivy: they were fortifications. Individual properties were walled, and so were communities. The word town is derived from the Old English *tun*, an enclosed place. The oldest town yet discovered, which is near the modern city of Jericho—famous for walls knocked down by the armies of Joshua—was surrounded by a wall of stones as early as 8000 B.C.

Towns were once walled both to keep enemies out and to enclose enough green space to feed the population during a siege. The garden wall that is most like a fortification today is the one intended to exclude one's fellow citizens. This is the wall around the front of the house, not just the back. It occurs in economies as apparently diverse as Haiti's and Hollywood's and in places as different as palaces and tourist resorts—wherever class distinctions are important. The relatively rich choose to wall themselves inside not only their houses but the surrounding grounds as well.

This kind of wall slices society into two parts. Outside the wall, it may be noisy, dusty and busy, a place for graffiti and garbage.

Inside may be a world of soft grass, water fountains, fragrant roses, professional gardeners and very few other people. The wall itself, seen from the inside, may be a cascade of flowering vines or may be barely visible behind trees and shrubs that soften the lines of brick and stone. What may be seen from the outside is barbed wire or broken glass on top of the wall, signs that in a very real way, the boundary separating the more privileged from the less is not easily crossed.

Someone locked out of a garden, as Mary Lennox was, cannot help wondering what might be within. When one is inside a closed garden, however, one's freedom is restricted, no matter how beautiful the place may be. The story of the Garden of Eden represents just such a paradox. Adam and Eve were content in that most wondrous of places before they had knowledge,

How pleasant it was, that civilized life in our gardens, with its exchanges of courtesies and amenities between the kitchen-garden and the "floral," the shrubbery and the poultry-yard. What harm ever came over an espalier trained along a party-wall whose coping-stones, held together with lichen and glowing yellow stonecrop, served as a promenade for toms and she-cats?
—Colette, Sido, 1922

but they were innocent prisoners, held within walls and laws they could not comprehend. After they had gained the ability to make judgements, they were forced to leave the garden, never to return. The gate was guarded by a sentry. No compromise was possible between life inside the garden and life outside the garden.

The Garden of Eden is the closed garden, the *hortus conclusus*, a metaphor used centuries ago to describe the Virgin Mary, with her unassailable innocence. The metaphor comes from the Song of Solomon: "A garden enclosed is my sister, my spouse; a spring shut up, a fountain sealed." The story of the life of the Buddha also begins with a sort of *hortus conclusus*. A child of wealthy parents, he was kept ignorant but physically satisfied within the walls of his family's privilege. Only when he became troubled by the suffering caused by poverty, illness and ageing did he leave the family estate to find his answers—his enlightenment—beyond the the walls. In the novel *The Secret Garden*, the closed garden is a metaphor for the locked heart. As the characters in the novel become more loving and whole, the garden is opened and returns to the full life it had lost with the death of the woman for whom it was created.

An open gate, of course, makes all the difference in a wall. Harry Symons writes, "A gap in a fence is like a breach in a fortification—

it makes the rest of the enclosure ineffective." It makes the enclosure ineffective as a fortification, that is, but not as a garden. The Ming dynasty writer Ch'iu Chian provided a refreshing perspective on the dilemma of the boundary, though he was talking about state borders, not garden walls. Where heaven has neglected the job of providing boundaries, he said, humanity must build them. Heavenly boundaries are natural features such as mountains and rivers. Ch'iu observed that since morality is the only difference between civilization and barbarism, people must remember that there is no sense building walls to protect a government which is not virtuous. The goodness or rightness of the boundary consists not in what it is, then, but in what it does. And nothing tempers what a wall does like a gate.

It may be selfish to hide so much beauty from general view; but until our dwelling-houses are made with uncurtained glass walls, that all the world may see everything, let those who have ample grounds enclose at least a portion for the sight of friends only.
—*Alice Morse Earle,* Old-Time Gardens, *1901*

Given this kind of thinking, it is not surprising that garden walls are common in China, where they are appreciated as beautiful objects in themselves. The *Yüan Yeh*, a Chinese landscaping book of 1634, advises: "Paper and pulp and chalk have of old been used for plastering the walls. Connoisseurs, who wished to give the walls a glossy surface, used for this purpose white wax, which they rubbed or patted into the wall. Today one uses for the ground yellow sand from rivers or lakes, mixed with a small quantity of chalk of the best quality, and over the whole is spread a little chalk as a covering surface. If this is rubbed carefully with a hempen brush, a mirror-bright surface will be produced." Vines never disguise these walls. They might have, however, variously shaped windows that turn the view of the world outside into so many moving pictures. These walls might be backdrops for vegetation or large stones or the shadows of objects and pavilions in the garden.

The same kind of untroubled appreciation of the garden wall extended into Japan, where in 1894, Lafcadio Hearn, a British-born journalist, wrote a description of his own very private garden in Tokyo in his *Glimpses of Unfamiliar Japan*: "There is nothing to break the illusion, so secluded the garden is. High walls and fences shut out streets and contiguous things; and the shrubs and the trees, heightening and thickening toward the boundaries, conceal from view even the roofs of the neighbouring katchiu-yashiki.

Softly beautiful are the tremulous shadows of leaves on the sunned sand; and the scent of flowers comes thinly sweet with every waft of tepid air; and there is a humming of bees."

Inside the walls can be much more pleasant than outside. That is why walled gardens are traditional in hot, sunny places, where they provide the most basic of mercies, shade. Walls also act as windbreaks, and they keep out noise and the business of the street. The walled mediaeval garden protected the calm confines of gentility, especially feminine gentility, from roaming livestock, drifting dust and the intrusions of passersby. Convents and seminaries were cloistered behind high walls: temptations not seen were temptations resisted. Walls provide what

It is unchristian to hedge from the sight of others the beauties of nature which it has been our good fortune to create or secure, and all the walls, high fences, hedge screens and belts of trees and shrubbery which are used for that purpose are so many means by which we show how unchristian and unneighbourly we can be.
—*Frank J. Scott*, Suburban Home Grounds, *1879*

might be very welcome privacy. The Japanese poet Tao Yuanming wrote: "In full light of day, I firmly shut my gate and debar all worldly thoughts from these bare rooms."

In a recent survey in Germany, most people described gardens as places where they could be undisturbed by their neighbours. There, as in much of Europe and Britain, walling gardens is customary. In cities, a wall-conscious practice of horticulture makes sense. Vertical gardening is a way of increasing the charm of these small spaces while compounding the surface area that can support vegetation.

The walled garden, even if it is as small as a balcony or porch, is then treated as an outdoor room of the house, open to the sky. Garden designers have worked with this idea for centuries. More than three hundred years ago, Sir William Temple suggested that the various compartments of a garden should be "like rooms out of which you step into another." Some of these spaces may be defined by only a subtle change in design, like the edge of a bed, lawn or patio, or there may be a wall but it may be simply decorative, like a boxwood hedge or a picket fence, with no pretensions of keeping out even the family cat. Landscaping then becomes a kind of outdoor version of interior decoration. Lawns and patios are floors, paths are hallways, benches and sculptures are furnishings, boundaries are walls, gates are doors. Floors are seldom level, of course, walls may curve, and furnishings may be nonexistent, but the concept can still help guide a designer who wants the garden to be as useful as possible. Allen Paterson, former director of the Royal Botanical Gardens in Ontario, writes: "The garden can be seen as a series of interconnected rooms with different uses and pleasures at various times of the day or year. Individual plants or groups of plants, though chosen, I hope, with care, are of rather less significance than the design as a whole. A garden is then like a big, living, three-dimensional walk-through sculpture inhabited by plants and people."

I know of one man in the neighbourhood who could give me valuable hints in the care of a garden, although he could not improve my knowledge of human nature. For instance, although he has put up a sign, "Please keep this gate shut," it has never been shut by anyone but himself. If he would only alter the words and make the sign read, "Please leave this gate open," it would always be shut and save him much worry and trouble.
—W.H. Davies, My Garden, 1933

Unfortunately, undefined garden spaces are often not used. The North American nervousness about seeming unsociable has helped produce miles of front-yard lawns that no one sits in or lies down on. In societies where garden walls are more common, they are not particularly offensive when the outside of one wall is the inside of the next-door neighbour's, and so on down the street. A row of houses may have a connecting row of walled gardens, which may be small but are intensely planted and frequently used. In Colette's 1922 book, *Sido*, the novelist recalls her childhood love of her family's walled garden in Paris: "I could gain my liberty at any moment by means of an easy climb over a gate, a wall, or a little sloping roof, but as soon as I landed back on the gravel of our own garden, illusion and faith returned to me. For as soon as she had asked me: 'Where have you come from?' and frowned the ritual frown, my mother would resume her placid, radiant garden-face, so much more beautiful than her anxious indoor-face. And merely because she held sway there and watched over it all, the walls grew higher, the enclosures which I had so easily traversed by jumping from wall to wall and branch to branch became unknown lands, and I found myself once more among the familiar wonders."

In North America, "good fences make good neighbours," as Robert Frost's neighbour said in the poem "Mending Wall," but only when they are hidden in the backyard. American botanist, teacher, horticulturist and writer L.H. Bailey advised around the turn of this century: "Front fences, in particular, are rarely desirable. The street and the walk sufficiently define the place…a real fence is more in keeping in a rear yard, for that yard is usually most in danger of molestation. In the backyard, the fence may become also a screen and a shelter. Usually it can be covered with vines—sometimes with grape vines—to advantage or be 'planted out' with bushes and trees. It is good practice to allow the fence to obtrude itself as little as possible."

The fence obtrudes not at all when it is invisible. One of the most welcoming ways to suggest a boundary without any sort of fence or wall is by using a gate on its own. Gardeners who want vertical surfaces for vines but do not want walls have taken to using arbours, arches and gates, some of which copy the Japanese *torii*, a gate that divides the sacred ground of the Shinto temple from the world that surrounds it but is not part of a tangible wall. It consists of straight uprights supporting one or two straight or curved horizontals. One of the most striking, built in the sea around the year 600, welcomes seagoing travellers to the temple at Miyajima. Any garden archway offers the same welcoming gesture. Although there are no walls alongside it, visitors, given the choice, almost always choose to go through the gate, not around it. To ignore the passage through the arbour would be like refusing an extended hand. One anticipates, too, sensual pleasures within the archway itself: a moment of shade, the smell of wisteria, the sight of bunches of fattening grapes.

Something there is that doesn't love a wall,
That sends the frozen-ground-swell under it,
And spills the upper boulders in the sun;
And makes gaps even two can pass abreast.
—Robert Frost, "Mending Wall," 1913

At the heart of the design concept that treats the landscape like a series of outdoor rooms is the house. Its walls are available to almost every gardener, and they come without any moral shadows. Vita Sackville-West, whose famous garden at Sissinghurst, England, is a wealth of walls and their living counterpart, hedges, wrote in one of her columns for *The Observer*: "Often I hear people say, 'How lucky you are to have these old walls; you can grow anything against them,' and then when I point out that every house means at least four walls—north, south, east and west—they say, 'I never thought of that.' " Of course, having four walls does not necessarily mean four places to plant vines. For vines, there must be decent soil at the base of the wall and no porch or walkway or foundation plants in the way. There must be at least a little sun, preferably a few hours of it. Any wall will, however, be a backdrop for the garden.

121

And it can be a backdrop for almost anything, as Sackville-West says. A bare wall may be a thing of beauty in a Chinese or Japanese garden, but in an English garden, it seems like an opportunity lost. The reason visitors to Old World gardens such as Sissinghurst are so taken with the walls is that the gardeners have used them so effectively. Many of Sackville-West's garden columns for *The Observer* were about plants for walls. She recommended magnolias, camellias and cotoneaster for the sides that faced north and west. "On the east side, which catches the morning sun, you can grow practically any of the hardy shrubs or climbers." South-facing walls in cool climates are the safest places for relatively tender fruits. Best able to take advantage of the reflected warmth of sunny walls are the two-dimensional trees known as espalier. They are so sheltered and warmed by the proximity of the wall that they may survive in a climate that would normally be too cold. For the south side, Sackville-West liked the idea of a grape vine, also one of Gertrude Jekyll's favourites.

This wall took 27 years out of my life. It's about a half-mile long, and it took maybe two million stones to build. It's over 6 feet tall and mostly 7 feet wide at the bottom.
—Albert (Stonewall) Johnson, Smiley, Saskatchewan

Jekyll wrote: "In my own home…prevailing wall-growths are vines and figs in the south and west and, in a shady northward-facing court between two projecting wings, *Clematis montana* on the two cooler sides and again a vine upon the other. At one angle on the warmer side of the house where the height to the eaves is not great, China roses have been trained up, and rosemary, which clothes the whole foot of the wall, is here encouraged to rise with it."

For most gardeners, vines and climbers are reason enough to garden close to walls, fences, pergolas, arbours, even hedges, shrubs and trees. Vines are some of the fastest-growing plants in the garden. Their tendency to clothe hard surfaces with soft greenery gives them a textural advantage in the garden design. Most of them flower, an additional virtue. Some flower spectacularly, like hybrid clematis, the cup-and-saucer vine, climbing nasturtium, sweet pea, black-eyed Susan vine, moonflower and, probably the easiest of an easy lot, the morning glory.

There are several ways vines make their way up almost anything even slightly inclined. All are sensitive to touch, a property called thigmotropism. What causes the plant to grow toward the place where contact has been made by a tendril or stem is the accelerated multiplication of cells on the side of the stem away from the contact. Plants such as morning glories spiral around slender supports and will even climb blades of grass until they flop over. Clematis has leaf stems that twine like fingers, allowing the central stem to remain relatively straight. Climbers such as sweet peas have modified leaf stems called tendrils, which do not produce leaves but may wind as tightly as coiled springs. In experiments at the University of Maryland, vines with tendrils turned out to be best adapted to low light conditions. These vines cannot hang on to bare walls, but others can. These so-called clingers include Virginia creeper, Boston ivy and climbing hy-

Envision the hole in the air that the wall makes, then fill it. A perfect wall would look as if it had been poured from concrete—and would be perfectly unsatisfying. Gives you nothing but dimension, says the Irishman. I'm speaking of dry wall, of course; mortar takes the interest right out of it.
—John Jerome, Stone Work, *1989*

drangea. Such plants have adhesive discs that attach to even the smoothest wall, while another clinger, ivy, has adventitious roots that penetrate and expand in cracks with such insistence that they can cause considerable damage to walls, bark, fences and masonry. Scandent plants, such as climbing roses, have long, slender branches that must be tied to a support.

Climbing roses, recommended by Jekyll and probably the most romantic of all wall plants, grew in abundance in the secret garden of Frances Hodgson Burnett's novel. In the fashion of most Victorian children's stories, the details, such as the tangle of climbing roses, were less important than the moral of the tale, but the book nevertheless presents a realistic example of the exuberant possibilities of confined horticulture, the sort of picture Burnett must have remembered from her childhood in England and the sort gardeners still aim for whether or not they can grow climbing roses. She breathlessly describes the effect of the garden on one of *The Secret Garden's* most soul-sick characters, the bedridden Colin Craven: "And over walls and earth and trees and swinging sprays and tendrils the fair green veil of tender little leaves had crept, and in the grass under the trees and the grey urns in the alcoves and here and there everywhere were touches or splashes of gold and purple and white and the trees were showing pink and snow above his head and there were fluttering of wings and faint sweet pipes and humming and scents and scents. And the sun fell warm upon his face like a hand with a lovely touch."

The garden perceived as a room open to the sky presents the gardener with this kind of possibility. Once our space is defined, we can concentrate our energy on producing something beautiful and useful within it. How accessible this beauty is to the world depends on how we use our boundaries and the gates within them.

Living Walls

Books like *The Secret Garden* encourage gardeners to think of walls in terms of wisteria or climbing roses, plants that do best in a climate like that of England, where Frances Hodgson Burnett was born, or New England, where she settled. Thanks to plant-breeding programs in Canada, roses exist that will survive in much harsher places, and there are many other perennial vines and climbers that will as well. Some of these are species of clematis, vines usually associated with fairly warm climates. The hardy species are smaller-flowered than the common purple *Clematis jackmanii* and the showier hybrids, but they are worth searching for, even for temperate gardens. Most are so scarce on this continent that they must be grown from seeds or from cuttings taken from a friend. The 1994 catalogue of Thompson & Morgan (P.O. Box 1308, Jackson, New Jersey 08527-0308) offers six types of seed.

Several perennial vines are mainstays for covering walls with greenery. English ivy (*Hedera helix*), where hardy, and the tougher Virginia creeper (*Parthenocissus quinquefolia*) or its cousin Boston ivy (*P. tricuspidata; Ampelopsis veitchii*), champion of the "ivy-league" schools, will cover a brick wall and may take over the garden if allowed to. Other good perennial vines include Dutchman's pipe (*Aristolochia durior*); trumpet vine (*Campsis radicans; Bignonia radicans*); American bittersweet (*Celastrus scandens*); climbing hydrangea (*Hydrangea petiolaris*); silverlace (*Polygonum aubertii*); grapes (*Vitis* spp), which become very heavy when fruiting, so need sturdy support; honeysuckle, from the hardy *Lonicera sempervirens*, with scarlet flowers, to the less hardy woodbine (*L. periclymenum*), with sweetly scented white flowers, and *L. japonica*, which has a longer blooming period.

Annual vines are cheaper because they can be grown from seed. They are also more adaptable because they can put up with places where winters are long and cold, provided there are enough frost-free days to allow them to flower for a few weeks. They do, of course, need to be replaced every year, but this also means they can be moved from place to place. Sweet peas have the unusual ability, for an annual vine, of preferring cool soil for germination and being tolerant of frost, much like garden peas.

Morning glories, moonflowers (*Ipomoea alba*), canary creeper vines (*Tropaeolum peregrinum*), black-eyed Susan vines (*Thunbergia alata*) and hyacinth beans (*Dolichos lablab*) are a few frost-tender possibilities that can also be grown from seed planted directly in the garden. They require only about three months of warmth and sun to reward the gardener with beautiful flowers. Climbing versions of vegetables such as snap beans, peas and cucumbers produce about twice as much food as bush varieties per plant, and the fruit is also much easier to pick.

The garden was a wide enclosure, surrounded with walls so high as to exclude every glimpse of prospect; a covered verandah ran down one side, and broad walks bordered a middle space divided into scores of little beds: these beds were assigned as gardens for the pupils to cultivate, and each bed had an owner.
—Charlotte Brontë, Jane Eyre, 1847

Most of the vines I grow are annuals because I appreciate their versatility and colour and because I have almost no place, yet, to grow perennials. Other than sweet peas, annual vines are tropical beauties that grow with all the vigour one would expect of jungle natives. My faith in their tenacity was renewed last year when I inherited half a dozen 'Heavenly Blue' morning glories whose seeds had been sown in juice-concentrate cans full of ordinary soil. The cans had no drainage, and the plants, grown indoors by a window, were already pale, overgrown and tangled up with each other when I got them in June. I extricated their roots with difficulty and planted them with resignation, but every one survived to bright blue splendour. The moonflower is the late-afternoon-blooming version of the morning glory. It is milky white, bigger and more sultry than its cousin. Both will climb anything slender.

The moonflower and morning glory can be sown directly outdoors, but there are a few annual vines I start early indoors. One is the bottle gourd (*Lagenaria* spp), because I want not just its white flowers, which are nice enough, but also the hard-shelled gourds that take much longer to mature. These plants should be started a month early—I use recycled plastic foam coffee cups or cardboard 1-litre (1-quart) milk cartons, cut down to a few inches tall, which can be ripped off at transplanting time. Cup-and-saucer vines (*Cobaea scandens*) are best given an indoor start too, because they take a long time to get going. I also start indoors some of the more unusual vines such as canary creeper, balloon vine (*Cardiospermum halicacabum*) and creeping gloxinia (*Asarina* spp), but when I have lost these vines to a late frost and sown replacements directly outdoors in warm soil, they have grown more quickly. A couple of annual vines that really should be started indoors about two months early —their seeds are small, so early growth is slow—are the purple bell vine (*Rhodochiton atrosanguineum*) and the Chilean glory flower (*Eccremocarpus scaber*). Both are delicate vines with fairly small flowers, best for hanging baskets.

My difficulty in growing vines is that the best windowless expanses of house wall rise from patios or pathways or behind dense foundation plantings. But I like vines, so I have found all kinds of ways to give them the vertical support they need. I have tied strings from a window ledge to the ground, propped trellises against the walls and put in an arbour. I have wrapped chicken wire around the trunk of a tree and threaded guiding strings through shrub branches. I have grown vines over stumps and piles of rocks and in hanging baskets and sconces. The desire for vertical elements in the garden seems to inspire all sorts of innovations so that even the gardener who lacks good walls can have vines. Whatever the vine, plant it at least 30 centimetres (1 foot) from the house wall. Closer than that is in the rain shadow, and a plant rooted there will need constant watering.

On Sex

I know a woman who not only is a gardener but also hosts a phone-in gardening show and owns a nursery business. Naturally, she likes to try new products. Last year, she bought a pheromone trap, one of the newest scientific approaches to the age-old problem of caterpillars in gardens. Tapping into the even older power of sex, the trap is designed to lure in male gypsy moths using the scent of females. A trapped male means trapped sex. Marjorie set up the pheromone trap according to the directions, but as she walked away, she says, "Suddenly there were moths flying around me and landing on me. At first, I didn't understand what was happening. I looked down and saw I was covered with gypsy moths and realized I must have spilled some of the pheromone on myself." What she had become was the irresistible object of moth desire.

This is the kind of desire that turns a pair of gypsy moths into 100 to 800 eggs and into enough bristly caterpillars to defoliate a forest. This kind of sexuality turns an acre of purple loosestrife into 24 billion seeds and a single aphid into 600 billion after nine generations. The mathematics of insect-pest sex and its botanical equivalent, weed sex, can be enough to make a gardener feel utterly bereft of control. A male moth can be drawn from a garden a couple of blocks away by as little as one-billionth of a gram of female pheromone. March flies, which appear in the northeastern part of the continent just as the snow melts, can copulate without interruption for as long as 56 hours, "a feat made more impressive by the fact that they as adults live only for two to five days," says Adrian Forsyth in his fascinating book, *A Natural History of Sex*. Spring, when Marjorie set up her moth trap, is the season "sweet lovers love," says Shakespeare, but it is also the season when everything else is focusing its lusty intentions upon others of its kind. Frogs begin to croak, birds to sing, snakes to slither and flowers to bloom, as brightly coloured and deliberately provocative as the rumps of baboons in heat. The Romans called the garden a *locus amoenus*—a lovely place, and a place for loving.

The great and amorous sky curved over the earth,
and lay upon her as a pure lover.
The rain, the humid flux descending from heaven
for both man and animal, for both thick and strong,
germinated the wheat, swelled the furrows with fecund mud
and brought forth the buds in the orchards.
And it is I who empowered these moist espousals,
I, the great Aphrodite…
—Aeschylus, The Danaides, c. 500 B.C.

But love and sex are such different things. Insect sex and plant sex inspire the humans in the garden to respond with chemicals so deadly they endanger not only the insects and plants but us too. And the hugeness of the insect and weed rebound is such that resistance to chemicals sometimes begins in a matter of months. Only a couple of eggs out of a thousand have to survive to adulthood for the species to prevail.

Given all this, it should not have surprised me to learn that the ancient Greek god of gardens was Priapus. Yet I admit that I expected someone more lovely and more loving to represent the garden. While many other fertility gods and goddesses are involved with agriculture and plants, Priapus is described, more clearly than anybody else, as the god who oversees the garden. His image, devoid of its huge phallus, his *magnito membri virilis*, has become the modern scarecrow. Neither handsome, pleasant nor loving, Priapus is foolish, quarrelsome and taken to chasing goddesses, who run from him with such desperation that they are hidden by other, more sympathetic deities. That is how the goddess Lotis became the flower lotus. Priapus' mother, Aphrodite, who was the most beautiful of goddesses and linked with fertility and sexuality herself—aphrodisiacs are her namesake, for one thing—disowned her ugly, awkward deformed child.

Evolutionary biology is now uttering and seeking those forces that link us with all those that have being. If we can discover the meaning in the trilling of a frog, perhaps we may understand why it is for us not merely noise but a song of poetry and emotion.
—*Adrian Forsyth,* A Natural History of Sex, *1986*

Not exactly a model of kindness, Aphrodite was, I like to think, something like the butterfly, moth or beetle that has nothing to do with its unbeautiful offspring. Cutworms, cabbage loopers, potato beetle larvae and leaf rollers are a few of the grubby children of pretty winged parents. Parsley worms are spotted and striped, but their showiness cannot hold a candle to the beauty of their mothers and fathers, the swallowtail butterflies. Stand very still in a tomato patch in summer, and you may hear the soft rain of droppings from the finger-thick tomato hornworms, the leaf-fraying sausage offspring of the hawkmoths that flutter among the moonflowers on warm evenings. Like Priapus, these larvae bear little resemblance to their mothers. Also like Priapus, they are the slaves of a single overriding passion. These unlovely babies are obsessed, however, with nothing but food. It is a brief passion aimed at taking them to adulthood, with its own overriding drive for sex. Along the way, they can more or less wreck a garden, but not if I can learn to manage them, to understand them rather than fear them.

This is one of the greatest skills of gardening. I have to be able to work with the almost incredible abundance of insect and weed sex so that the garden can suit my idea of the *locus amoenus*. Some kind of compromise is necessary. Priapus is all sex, no romance, and that may be fine for the insects, but it was not good enough for Lotis, and it is not enough for me. I don't want the tatters of leaves, all that is left after the passions of the butterflies have been played out in my cabbages, and I don't want beds full of weeds. But I also don't

131

want the overkill that comes with so many chemical cures. I have to learn to set traps and scrape off egg masses, I have to weed by hand or learn ways, like mulching, to keep weed seeds from germinating, and I have to learn about the sprays that are selective for certain troublesome things and will not leave dangerous residues behind.

The principle of agriculture is the principle of ordered sexual union.
—*Johann Jakob Bachofen, 1861*

If the garden is a sexual place for me, it is because I want it to woo me. It must beguile and flirt and fascinate. It has to offer me flowers and perfumes. One of the half-brothers of Priapus, Cupid—another son of Aphrodite, who was as irresistible to the gods as a female pheromone to a male moth—is more in keeping with the garden as a place of romance. Cupid is, for us, the flying baby with the arrows, but the Greeks saw more clearly his aphrodisiac bloodlines. He was a handsome young god who hunted people and stung them with his arrows of desire. His connection with Valentine's Day, with its sensual bright reds and its boxes of bright roses, is an old one. Valentine's Day comes too early to have much to do with northern gardens, and it has even less to do with its namesake, a Roman priest martyred for sheltering persecuted Christians. St. Valentine's name was glued onto what had been, in the Mediterranean climate where the festival originated, a time to honour the mating of birds. No early festival was entirely about nature, however; festivals were really about the human connection with nature. St. Valentine's Day was a garden festival, so Priapus, too, took part.

Chaucer's *The Parlement of Foulys*—fowls, that is—is one of many mediaeval poems that celebrates St. Valentine's Day with an allegory of love involving birds and gardens. The narrator dreams he enters a beautiful garden that is designed to show both the happiness and the dangers which can come with love. First, the dangers: he is led by Cupid, his tour guide, to a temple that contains an image of Priapus, "his sceptre in honde," as well as a statue of Venus, "nakyd from the brest yp to the hede." The narrator leaves the temple, with its symbols of lusty sexuality, for the outdoors, where the songbirds have a discussion before the goddess of nature, "for this was on seynt Valentynys day." The birds are about to choose their mates, but three of them are in love with the same female, so they discuss how to resolve this problem in a courtly manner. The most honourable solution, the birds decide, means remaining chaste but faithful. It is a resolution that only a human being could dream up, but one that centuries of observers admired—believing they had seen it—in nature too, in the inner workings of beehives.

The sexual behaviour of honeybees, best loved of garden insects, did not go unnoticed by early Greeks and Romans, who saw in the death of the drone after mating with the queen a model of dedication and faithfulness. The remaining bees, which they mistook for males under the dominion of a king, lived asexually, devoted only to work. The poet Virgil wrote: "Let garden plots woo them with fragrance of their yellow flowers, and the watchman of thieves and birds, Hellespontic Priapus, keep them in guard with his hook

Then Heaven, the Father almighty, comes down in fruitful showers into the lap of his joyous spouse, and his might, with her mighty frame commingling, nurtures all growths.
—Virgil, Georgics, 1st century B.C.

of willow...they neither delight in bodily union, nor melt away in languor of love, nor bear their young by birth-throes." Their impressive show of chastity inspired some early Christian communities, who went so far as to ritually castrate themselves as a sign of devotion. Of course, the worker bee, like the gypsy moth larva, the cutworm, the baby bird and the human child, is not so much devoted to celibacy as to preparation for the critical sexual stage to come. The drone bee represents the entire hive when, for a short time, he pursues the queen with the energy of Priapus.

Flowers, like honeybees, have at times been considered organisms that exist beyond earthly sexuality—lilies and roses were once associated with the Virgin Mary, despite their seductive fragrances—but celibacy in nature is a death sentence; abundance means survival, and flowers are actually very expensive sexual lures, expensive in terms of the energy the plant devotes to them. Showy petals, strong perfumes and sweet nectars, some as much as four-fifths sugar, have a brief season to do a desperately important job. Pollination must take place, and seeds must be fertilized early enough to reach maturity while the weather permits. Flowers are the organs of plant sex, as eager as Priapus but as beautiful as Aphrodite—or perhaps Flora, another beauty, the Roman goddess of flowers.

There is an interesting side effect to the mistaken impression that flowers are simply nature's decorations. Women have often been compared to flowers—"my love is like a red, red rose," and so forth. Flower names have been given to women—Flora, Rose, Daphne,

Lily, Daisy, Myrtle, Heather and many more—but not because flowers are advertisements of sexuality. Sarah Josepha Hale was typical of her time and place, New England a century and a half ago, when she counselled women to "cultivate those virtues which can only be represented in the finest flowers." Pretty, silent, passive and perfumed, she meant. When the sexuality of flowers was put in graphic terms by the botanist Carl Linnaeus, who compared the numbers of stamens and pistils to various numbers of husbands or wives in a marriage, some people were horrified by the metaphor. What was going on among the lilies? The Reverend Samuel Goodenough wrote to the founder of the Linnaean Society in 1808: "A literal translation of the first principles of Linnaean botany is enough to shock female modesty."

Another day it occurred to me that time as we know it doesn't exist in a lawn, since grass never dies or is allowed to flower and set seed. Lawns are nature purged of sex or death. No wonder Americans like them so much.
—*Michael Pollan,* Second Nature, *1991*

Earlier, more agrarian societies were comfortable with the knowledge that petals pointed the way to ovaries full of seeds or surrounded stamens heavy with pollen. Anyone could see that all grains and fruits started out as flowers. After the petals and flowers fell, fruits and grains, which swelled like so many female bellies, were easy to identify with human sexuality. In Japan, Isao Uemichi says, "The shape and colour of a ripe peach suggest pregnancy, and in cryptology, it implies female reproductive organs." There, March 3, "Girl's Festival," is associated with the blooming of peaches, "symbolic of the coming of spring and the rosiness of maidens."

The peach is a member of a sensuous family, the roses. Before the rose was the flower of the Virgin Mary, it was claimed by the much more earthy Aphrodite and her Roman counterpart, Venus. These goddesses had not a shred of coyness, and they suited a time when the sexuality of nature and of people were known to be intimately connected. As naturalist Donald Culcross Peattie said in the 1930s of the sound of the first spring frog, "It tells of all that is most unutterable in evolution—the terrible continuity and fluidity of protoplasm, the irresistible forces of reproduction—not mythical human love, but the cold Bactrian jelly by which we humans are linked to things that creep and writhe and are blind yet breed and have being."

Semen is one of the forms of "cold Bactrian jelly" that was known to play a part in the pregnancy of people and animals. Generations

134

ago, it was compared to rain and its expression in plants, sap, which obviously encouraged plant growth and helped fruit swell. Fruit has long suggested pregnancy, but a more farfetched belief compared the plant's "seed head" to the human head. The brain was believed to be the seat of sexuality in a very different way from our present understanding that sex is governed by the hypothalamus and fuelled by the emotions. A belief, seemingly older than history, that semen originated in the head—the brain and spinal fluid look like the right sort of "cold Bactrian jelly"—endured until quite recently and influenced even people as learned as Leonardo da Vinci. Although his anatomical studies should have shown him that the supposed physical connection between the spinal cord and the testes, pipeline for brain power, did not exist, his belief overcame his reason.

From various parts of the world come stories about couples making love in newly sown fields, linking human and plant fertility. The Puritan writer Phillip Stubbes was shocked by the vestiges of this sort of ritual when he described May Day in 16th-century England. Part of the festivities had involved setting up the maypole, one of countless incarnations of the tree of life: "And thus beeing reared up, with handkercheefs and flags hovering on the top, they straw the ground rounde about, binde green boughes about it, set up sommer haules, bowers, and arbors hard by it. And then fall they to daunce about it, like as the heathen people did at the dedication of the Idols, whereof this is a perfect pattern, or rather the thing itself. I have heard it credibly reported (and that *viva voce*) by men of great gravitie and reputation, that of fortie, threescore or a hundred maides going to the wood over night, there have scaresly the third part of them returned home againe undefiled."

My own recollections of maypole dancing in Vancouver in the 1950s are very different. The poles were stored in the closets of the school gym from June to April, then pulled out for the fifth- and

Perhaps my unhappiest moment was the discovery in several catalogues of a combination of dwarfism and giantism in the person of "Miss Universe, a brand-new idea in zinnias. She has stems only 2 feet high and flowers 7 inches across." Poor Miss Universe! She reminds me of my own plight as a girl. I was short, with a great knot of hair at the back of my head. I had not particularly worried about my appearance, though, until an old friend of the family said to me, "I suppose you realize, my dear, that your hair is a deformity."

Remembering how I felt, I suggest that we do not deform flowers or, for that matter, dwarf the princesses.

—Katharine S. White, Onward and Upward in the Garden, *1958*

sixth-grade girls to learn to dance around. The steps were choreographed so that the ribbons attached to the top of the poles wove together. We knew nothing about fertility rites, and we didn't want to. All we worried about was learning the steps and not tripping or tangling our ribbons. We wanted to dance and have fun. But come to think of it, that is probably the way it was in Stubbes' England, too, and the way it has been since people first created rhythms and kicked up their heels. The meaning of the dance might matter to the priests, but for ordinary people what has mattered is the dance itself. The rhythm that resonates with life's vibrancy is there whether or not we know what it means.

If the allure of old roses is in the frank sensuality of their blooms, then what are we to make of the development and eventual triumph of the modern hybrid tea? Maybe the Victorian middle class simply couldn't deal with the rose's sexuality.
—Michael Pollan, Second Nature, 1991

The female followers of Bacchus, the Roman god of wine, counterpart of the Greek Dionysus, were the most frenzied of dancers. The male followers of the handsome god were satyrs—half-goat, half-human gods whose name is given to satyriasis, excessive sexual desire—and the females were bacchantes, or maenads, best known for their wild dancing, an expression of the most primal life force. Their poses, frozen in midair, decorate ancient vases and walls. Bacchus is also one of the garden gods, especially of gardens draped and shaded by grape vines.

Because sexual energy was believed to be concentrated in the head, male beards and the horns of animals seemed to be expressions of overflowing fertility and vitality—satyrs had horns, and so did Dionysus. Animal horns are still precious aphrodisiacs in China, however endangered a particular species might be. The moon, too, passes through a crescent stage when it looks horned, which suggested a link with fertility. The moon also seemed to create a mysterious liquid, dew, which was thought to restore the vitality of plants. Foliage that had been limp and dry at the end of a hot day was firm and damp in the morning. Furthermore, the moon waxes and wanes with the 28-day rhythm of women's fertility—hence *mens*, moon, leads to the word menstruation.

All of these signals pointed to a close link between the moon and the flourishing of life. The waxing of the moon in spring, like the swelling of pregnancy, is an ancient signal for the time to sow seeds. Thomas Hill wrote in *The Gardener's Labyrinth* of 1577:

"What seed the Gardener mindeth to commit, in a well dressed earth, let these be bestowed from the first day until the full light of the Moon (well nigh) for that seeds sown in the wane of the Moone come up thin, and the plants insue weake of growth." The full moon was, of course, the time to pick fruit, while grains were harvested and trees cut when the moon was waning. In an age when clocks and calendars were clumsy and scarce, the moon was the most dependable chart for garden routines throughout the season, and every full moon had its instructional label; the one closest to the fall equinox at the end of September was the harvest moon. Advice about planting, sowing, pruning and harvesting by the phase of the moon is still published every year in *The Farmer's Almanac*. A happy coincidence for writers of romantic songs in the English language is the rhyming of moon with June, because the connections between love, fertility, the moon and beauty are ancient ones.

In England, both men and women are moved by the grace of gardens and of landscapes, but although the roses are allowed to climb upon the walls of houses, I have rarely seen an Englishwoman dare to put a rose in her hair. To her, this would seem inappropriately seductive. Aphrodite must stay in the garden, but there she is honoured without anxiety, without limits.
—Ginette Paris, Pagan Meditations, *1986*

Innana, a fertility goddess, is one of the oldest Eurasian deities of the moon, especially the crescent moon. Her name branched into that of many other goddesses—Ishtar, Astarte, Ashtaroth, perhaps Esther of the Old Testament—and she is an early version of Aphrodite and Venus. Innana was both sensual and sexual, a goddess of fertility and beauty.

There are records, written in stone, of fertility celebrations that took place about 5,000 years ago in what is now the southern part of Iraq, where the Sumerians built a complex society of cities and farms. The sacred marriage of Innana with Dumuzi, the shepherd god of vegetation, later known as Tammuz, was celebrated every year by the union of the real king with a representative of Innana. Dumuzi, like many deities concerned with plants, died and was reborn every year, fetched back from the underworld by Innana. Their reunion was celebrated with rapturous love songs written in language reminiscent of the biblical Song of Solomon. A poet wrote that the bride considered the king "honey of my eyes, the lettuce of my heart"—lettuce, green, tender and lush, was a cherished food—and said that after the couple made love, "At the king's lap stood the rising cedar, / Plants rose high by his side, / Grains rose high by his side, / ... [and] gardens flourished luxuriantly by his side."

Another poem expressed the thoughts of Innana and the concept, at least as old as agriculture, that the earth is female, while the tools that work it are male: "As for me, my vulva, / For me the piled-high hillock, / Me, the maid, who will plow it for me? / My vulva, the watered ground—for me, / Me, the Queen, who will station the ox there?"

Let no one on Midsummer Day or on certain solemn occasions honoring the Saints practise the observation of the solstices, dances, carols and diabolical songs.
—*Saint Eloi, 7th century*

The answer follows: "O Lordly lady, the king will plow it for you, / Dumuzi, the king, will plow it for you."

This graphic sensuality lingered for centuries, in reality or in reputation, in the gardens of the east. Western European crusaders and wealthy travellers alike brought home to their cabbage patches and apple orchards stories of eastern gardens behind whose high walls were fragrant flowers, sweet fruits, cool fountains—flowing, perhaps, with honey or wine—and beautiful women. These were the gardens of male fantasy. Persia was the presumed location of the Garden of Eden, so it was only to be expected that copies of paradise, complete with temptations, might still be found there.

In the Middle Ages, Marco Polo told a story of a Persian chief's garden whose entire purpose was a fulfilment of all the senses, in imitation of the garden of paradise that awaited good Muslim men after death. This chief's hidden garden—which Polo admitted to having heard about but not seen—had devices that produced streams of honey, wine, milk and water, as well as palaces throughout. "The inhabitants of these palaces were elegant and beautiful damsels, accomplished in the arts of singing, playing upon all sorts of musical instruments, dancing and especially those of dalliance and amorous allurement." The chief wanted to impress the populace without giving away his garden's location, so he drugged young men with opium and had them carried in. When the youths awoke, they found themselves receiving "the most fascinating caresses" from the women. These were the earthly version of the houris, beautiful, eternally youthful women who attend to men in paradise.

To Europeans schooled to believe in a celibate heaven, such a vision smacked of immorality, yet they longed to know more. They designed their gardens in the foursquare form of the east, and they sought to grow the tulips, roses, camellias and oranges that brought with them the colours, fragrances and flavours of foreign sensuality. There was more to come. From 16th-century Arabia came a medicinal guide to sexual matters and aphrodisiacs, *The Perfumed Garden*, which was banned from publication in English-speaking countries until this century. According to the book, which was more medicinal than titillating, desire in women could be enhanced by orchis, carrot seed, turnip seed, pulverized burnt nasturtium, powdered willow leaves and the piths of fine dates. The English, meanwhile, had put their trust in the bean flower, whose fragrance "not only stimulates passion in the man but extreme willingness in the girl."

Adam the while
Waiting desirous her return, had wove
Of choicest flow'rs a garland to adorn
Her tresses, and her rural labours crown,
As reapers oft are wont their harvest-queen.
—*John Milton,* Paradise Lost, *1667*

An eastern aphrodisiac of a very different sort was introduced to England in 1718 by Lady Mary Wortley Montagu, who described a language of symbols supposedly used by members of Turkish harems for secret communication with lovers other than the sultan. The code's symbols included a variety of objects, such as matches ("I burn, I burn, my flame consumes me") and straw ("Suffer me to be your slave") as well as flowers such as roses ("May you be pleased, and all your sorrows mine"). The idea ignited into a craze in western Europe, but only the flowers were retained. Soon, every flower in the garden had its meaning, from monkshood ("knight errantry") to marigold ("indifference"), and meanings were apt to change from author to author. More of flirtation than passion remained in the westerly version of the language of the Turkish harems, and now it was possible to communicate disdain rather than acceptance. A lover's advances could be refused with a sprig of nightshade. Nobody dared to suggest, however, that roses meant anything other than love or desire —a dozen for Valentine's Day was always a safe bet—but depending upon the colour and maturity of the bloom, the message might carry subtleties such as innocence or anguish.

The language of flowers lives on today in quaint little books that still appear every Christmas. And there is another version that passes between plant breeder and gardener. It is the code of cultivar names. Here, too, a certain sensuality still clings to some flowers, especially roses. A rose is a rose is a rose, as Gertrude Stein said, but a rose is something more than simply a circle of petals when it is called 'Belle Amour' or 'Dusky Maiden,' two of the older names. Another rose of past centuries is 'Maiden's Blush'—also known as 'Cuisse de Nymphe,' thigh of a nymph. This rose "seems to press her sexuality upon us," says Michael Pollan, editor of *Harper's Magazine*, who confesses in his book *Second Nature* that he could not believe a name could be so appropriate until he experienced it in his own Connecticut garden: "These nymph thighs ...this unmistakable carnality." Twentieth-century rose breeders took a giant step away from sensuality when they concentrated on long-lasting blooms instead of fragrance, but a few cultivar names in a 1994 nursery catalogue show that breeders are on the same old track. There were 'Dolce Vita,' 'La Passionata' and, best of all, a rose simply called 'Woman': "Graceful sculptured buds have a delicate ivory base and pink flush towards the centre. A tall-growing rose, exquisitely perfumed."

A little gluttony as regards fruit is so natural! As to myself, I cannot honestly deny, and therefore frankly confess, that I sympathize with our mother Eve.
—*Cornelia J. Randolph,* The Parlor Garden, *1884*

I am just beginning to become a lover of roses. In my last garden, I favoured tough types that needed no winter protection. They were more like peasants than nymphs. 'Persian Yellow' bloomed sunny yellow for a few days in July but was so eager to prevail that it threatened to overwhelm its flowerbed. A few strains of the species *hansa* have given me fat, applelike hips after their flat pink flower petals fell. In my new garden, I planted a couple of David Austen's new English roses, which are gorgeous and reputed to be a little hardier than some of the heirlooms. The bright yellow 'Graham Thomas' did not survive its first winter, but the pink 'St. Cecilia' did. I purchased her for purely sentimental reasons—Cecilia is the patron saint of music—and now, in spring, no visit to the garden is complete until I pay homage to her new unfolding leaves. It's been a long time since I have been so excited by the progress of a single plant.

In any case, my garden will not depend upon roses to be a place of sensuality and sexuality. Whatever I grow, the shadow of Aphrodite will linger just under the flower petals where the seeds wait to ripen, the laughter of Dionysus will sound in the territorial calls of blue jays, the dance of the maenads will be copied in the anthills and in clouds of pollen caught by the wind. The face of the moon will be a goddess of fertility. The uncontrollable passion of Priapus will inspire the moths and butterflies seeking their mates in my trees and flowers. If I can learn to live with this exuberant vitality, my garden can be a place for the two sons of Aphrodite, Cupid and Priapus, and it can be a place for me.

Survival Tactics

Caterpillars and dandelion seeds offer some of the more obvious signs of nature's procreative abundance, but there is also a sign within some of us, an invisible one. Although only one sperm is required to fertilize an egg, a millilitre (0.034 ounce) of human semen contains millions. More precisely, about 66 million, a figure that has attracted a lot of attention recently, not because it is so high but because it is so low. Just 30 years ago, one millilitre contained almost twice as many sperm, about 113 million. According to a 1992 report in the *British Medical Journal*, this precipitous tumble in a couple of generations is "more probably due to environmental rather than genetic factors."

A glimmer of optimism in this gloomy decline was recorded two years later in another British journal, *The Lancet*. A group of Danish organic farmers who ate only food grown without pesticides turned out to have around double the average sperm count. It was as though they had arrived at 1994 in a time machine that started its flight 30 years ago. The finding corroborated what organic gardeners and farmers have always maintained: pesticides harm not only pests—as well as wildlife and other creatures—but also ourselves. Many health problems, ranging from allergic reactions to death, can result from exposure to pesticides. Low sperm counts are less dramatic only because they are usually undetected: a man is unlikely to have a fertility problem unless his sperm count drops below 20 million.

Some of the blame for this small symptom of the enormous problem of pesticides in the environment can be laid at the rubber boots of home gardeners, who, in the United States at any rate, use more than four times as much pesticide as farmers, acre for acre. Furthermore, less than one-tenth of 1 percent is estimated to actually contact the target pest; the remainder contaminates soil, air and water. In 1990, the most common pesticide contaminant of wells in the United States was DCPA, a herbicide often used on lawns.

So what is a home gardener to do? First, stop buying pesticides and become more tolerant of imperfect-looking things in the garden. Spots and streaks won't hurt you, but the remedy might. Take a slow walk around the garden as often as you can so that you will spot problems as soon as they occur. When diseases or pests do show up, there are some benign methods of control or cure.

For pests, hand-picking, squishing, trapping and washing off—or burning off, in the case of tent caterpillars—are a few safe techniques. Dig or smother weeds. A spray of a small amount of dish soap in water or insecticidal soap applied according to package directions will kill a wide range on contact. It can be made stronger by adding plants that contain their own insecticides or deterrents: pressed garlic, cayenne and other herbs, chopped citrus peels.

Certain botanical pesticides will harm humans and other creatures as well, but they do have the attribute of breaking down swiftly into harmless ingredients after application. These include rotenone, pyrethrum and various others that become available from time to time. If you use them, be careful not to inhale them or let them contact your skin. Use them on a calm day and only where they are needed. Store them in a cool place out of the reach of children.

Several pest diseases are also on the market. The most common is *Bacillus thuringiensis* (Bt), sold in almost every garden store under a variety of brand names. Bt is a fatal disease of moth and butterfly larvae such as tomato hornworms, cabbage loopers, tent caterpillars and gypsy moth larvae. It must be sprayed directly on the caterpillars, which will then stop feeding and die in a couple of days. Again, the more carefully you can direct the spray, the better; Bt also kills the larvae of butterflies such as monarchs and swallowtails.

Plant diseases are usually harder to diagnose and treat. Dormant oils can be applied to fruit trees and shrubs before bud break in spring. A spray of 5 millilitres (1 teaspoon) of baking soda in a litre (a quart) of water helps reduce fungus problems such as black spot on roses; this is another case where the spray should be used as a preventive early in the season. Sometimes sick plants or parts of plants have to be destroyed. A few plants have well-known susceptibilities to certain diseases in certain parts of the continent. A good plant nursery will warn you about them. There may be pest-resistant strains of the plant, or you may choose to grow something more self-reliant. If signs of disease show up on annual plants—this often happens on vegetables such as tomatoes, potatoes and squashes—pull out the dead plants at season's end and dispose of them somewhere other than in the compost bin. Next year, try a different cultivar, perhaps one known for disease resistance.

We gardeners normally consider ourselves defenders of the beauty of the Earth, but when it comes to pesticide use, we can thoughtlessly do a lot of harm. The good news is that it is quite possible to garden successfully without pesticides, and organic practices benefit not only ourselves but, in a very direct way, generations yet unborn.

On Plants

Why can't plants walk? It sounds like a silly question. But given the extravagant possibilities of evolution, why *would* anything end up stuck in one place, subject to every whim of weather and climate, unable to run from fires or chain saws or browsing deer or children making bouquets? Why no legs, fins, wings for independent motion?

The rootedness of plants is at the very heart of the appeal of the garden. People are almost always on the move; gardens are not. Gardens are places where living things are there for us, waiting, accessible, whenever we want them. We do not have to make appointments with gardens. In fact, gardens were here before we were. Eden waited for Adam. Plants existed before animals, whose vast diversity can be explained, in part, by the enormous variety of environmental niches that plants presented. Creatures that could get about on their own steam could eat leaves, drink nectar, bore holes in trunks, consume seeds or make fingerling potato salads with raspberry vinegar and olive oil dressing. Plants are both food and shelter for things that fly, burrow, swim, crawl, slither and walk. For us, they are fuel both for our fires and for our inspiration.

In a strictly genetic sense, all organisms are unarguably of one family. Our numerous common features, especially at the molecular level, indicate at least a close cousinhood, a common descent from one or a few very similar ancestors.
—*Steven Vogel,* Life's Devices, *1988*

But what is in it for the plants? Is it their lot to be merely the rungs in our evolutionary ladder? Why can't they walk—or run—away from all this rampant consumerism?

If it is a silly question, it has a silly answer: plants do not walk because they do not need to. Why should they bother with that great investment of energy when they can get everything they need in one place? If they could, they might well wonder at all our frantic comings and goings. From where they sit, they net, gather, entice, grab, suck and probe. Thanks to a variety of adaptations, plants can bounce back, as species if not as individuals, from virtually anything that comes their way. They can fend off predators with smelly, bad-tasting oils, with poisons, irritants, thorns and barks. They can shed leaves in anticipation of difficult times. As seeds, they can survive fire and flood. Plants do become extinct, but that is not a sign of inherent weakness; more mobile things become extinct as well.

Another answer to the question exists: photosynthesis does not provide plants with enough energy for anything beyond a minimal level of independent movement. Plants are plenty busy in one spot. There, they are remarkably efficient at turning very little in the way of visible raw materials into a great deal of matter, a fact proved several centuries ago by van Helmont, a Swiss chemist. Van Helmont was astonished by the results of his own experiment. He put 91 kilograms (200 pounds) of dry soil in a container, moistened it and planted a 2.3-kilogram (5-pound) willow shoot in it. After five years of giving the willow nothing but rainwater, he weighed it and found that it was now 74 kilograms (164 pounds). The chemist then dried the soil, weighed it on its own and found that it was about 57 grams (2 ounces) lighter than five years earlier. "Thus," he wrote, "the 164 pounds of wood, bark and root arose from the water alone." We now know that the chemist's conclusions were not quite accurate; 164 pounds of willow came from the energy of sunlight acting with water, minerals and air. But the fact remains that plants live on what humans would consider much less than a starvation diet. Fifty-seven grams of food would maintain our body weight for less than a day.

What you forget is that plants themselves want to live as much as you want them to. More.
—*Elizabeth Smart,* Elizabeth's Garden, *1989*

Plants do move—shoots grow, seeds are flung out, roots reach into the soil, petals close on cloudy days, the leaves of carnivorous plants close around hapless insects—but they do not change location under their own power. During the stages in which motion away from the parent plant is necessary—shifting pollen from one plant to another or transporting seeds to new territory—plants borrow other things that have independent movement: fluids such as moving air and water and high-octane creatures such as insects, animals and humans. Plants ensure, to an uncanny extent, that these servants are well enough paid and carefully enough directed that they will do exactly what is necessary: take the perfectly ripe pollen from one apple blossom to another apple blossom; deposit the seeds from the raspberry, packed in a little bird-excrement fertilizer, by the hedgerow to germinate.

One might say that in addition to having no feet, plants have no brains, but plants, though undoubtedly brainless, are just as smart as they need to be. Not that they act with deliberation (well, probably not. Scientists shudder at anthropomorphic gardeners, but there is a temptation to think, well, that they think, sort of...), but plants have, obviously, done what they needed to do. They do not need to know how to fly or crawl, make honey or nests, sing or pole-vault, balance a chequebook or make spaceships. Instead, they offer the carbohydrates and proteins, the cellulose, fragrances and colours that allow those things to be done.

Plants are our calm earthly companions and, more than that, our complements. They are made from the same stuff as we are. They need air, food and water. They use the same minerals as we do. And they are composed of the same proteins, which break down if the temperature becomes too high, causing damage, then death. Their sexual reproduction method is similar to that of animals, with male cells having to make their way to a botanical womb that holds seeds which must be fertilized. The young are given a food supply by the parent to carry them through the initial struggle to establish an independent existence. Plants, like ourselves, have hormones that regulate growth and various stages of maturation. Plants are wounded and heal, they suffer from disease, they struggle, survive and die.

If you remarked how well a plant was looking, he would gravely touch his hat and thank you with solemn unction; all credit in the matter falling to him. If, on the other hand, you called his attention to some back-going vegetable, he would quote Scripture… all blame being left to Providence.
—R. L. Stevenson, Memories and Portraits, 1887

Nevertheless, plants are as distinct a life form from humans as any the Starship *Enterprise* might discover on its search through outer space. I remember the time I first came to the realization, as a child in a forest, that everything around me was as alive as I was. It is the sort of feeling that could easily be translated into horror. But plants are too different from us to be frightening in the manner of ants or mites seen under microscopes, with their odd legs and odd eyes and odd mouths. Plants just seem wonderful. And the more one knows about plants, the more wonderful these strange, though not alien, life forms seem. Plants cannot walk. They cannot vocalize. They dine on sunlight and spit out oxygen. Their blood is green or white or yellow, seldom red. Some of them, like the exuberant dandelion, can produce fertile seeds without fertilization, a process called parthenocarpy, from the Greek term for virgin birth. Capable of growing a complete copy of itself from a piece of itself, the humble dandelion might be a better flower to symbolize the Virgin Mary than the red rose or the Madonna lily. Some plants, like the walnut tree, can keep neighbouring roots at a distance by exuding or dripping chemicals into the soil. Some send out intoxicating fragrances to gather in the bees and moths. Some smell like rotting meat to gather in flies.

"Do what you do do well," go the words of a cautionary song, and it is advice plants follow. But they do what they do in their own way, not ours. The only ancestors that plants and humans have in common came into being at the beginning of the evolutionary path, hundreds of millions of years ago. One that is still around, turning stagnant ponds into green soup in summer, is the euglena, a tiny single-celled chlorophyll producer that is guided by a light-sensitive eyespot. It splits in two when it feels the urge to make more euglenas and has independent movement, thanks to a whipping tail.

But frankly, the euglena, along with algae, lichens and even mosses, also plants of ancient lineage, are not the plants most gardeners give much thought to. This is not necessarily a good thing. Some of the most beautiful Japanese gardens depend greatly upon the softening and ageing effect of various mosses in their countless shades and textures of green. The Nitobe garden in Vancouver has around 40 varieties, whose cushions and textures, mirrored in a pond, link rocks and earth visually with taller plants. But in most gardens, these simple green things are too still. We want action.

As an avid home gardener and mother of adopted children, I'm often struck with the parallels between these two absorbing lifetime occupations. Plants and children. We their nurturers provide the best home and the most growth-nurturing care that we know and are capable of at the time. But in the end, they both are going to do what they need to do.
—Helen Chesnut, October 1992

We want flowering and fruiting and, at the appropriate time, leaves that change colour and fall. Things that stay the same all year, though valuable in their place—junipers for foundation plantings, grasses mowed into lawns, mosses and lichens on rock walls, algae in ponds—become mere backdrops. The Occidental style of gardening demands a kind of dynamic tension: plants that are rooted but visibly changing. From plants, we want buds and shoots, blossoms and fruit, bouquets and bowers and even the sadness of falling petals. We depend on plants as much as the weather to tell us about the seasons, through perfumes and colours, through times of sprouting and harvest. Spring is yellow-green; summer is bright colours of every hue; fall is gold and red; winter is white, dark green and brown.

I was intrigued to learn that at one time (before Julius Caesar instated that peculiarly Roman form of linear thinking that straightjacketed the year into a dozen months), the months of the year were named for trees. There were 13 of them, in tune with the phases of the moon. Robert Graves, in his book *The Greek Myths*, writes that in ancient Ireland, each of the 13 months was named for a tree whose name was also that of one of the 13 consonants of the Irish alphabet. The five vowels represented the beginnings of the four seasons and, again, certain plants: O, gorse, for the spring

149

equinox; U, heather, for the summer solstice; E, poplar, for the fall equinox; and for the winter solstice, both A, fir, the birth tree, and I, yew, the death tree. Just as our alphabet is named for the first two letters of the Greek alphabet, alpha and beta, so the Irish alphabet was named for its first three consonants. It was called the Beth-luis-non, which means birch, rowan and ash. Graves writes: "This order of trees is also implicit in Greek and Latin myth and the sacral tradition of Europe and Asia Minor." The Greek goddess Themis, it was said, prescribed the 13-month year, divided by the solstices into two seasons, sprouting and wintering. Graves adds that the Irish alphabet was said to have come from Greece by way of Spain and that the current order of letters of Eurasian languages, beginning "A, B, C," may have been a deliberate misarrangement by Phoenician merchants devising a secret code for use in trade.

To see a world in a Grain of Sand
And a Heaven in a Wild Flower
Hold Infinity in the palm of your hand
And Eternity in an hour.
—William Blake, "Auguries of Innocence," 1863

It seems fitting to name months for trees, certainly more fitting than naming them after conquerors like the two Caesars, Julius (July) and Augustus (August). Would our world be different, I wonder, if we still had a year of 13 months, each of which had a full moon, each of which had its special tree? Trees, as the largest and most enduring of all living things on Earth, sturdily connecting the underworld with the heavens, enduring changes of season and generations of humanity while rooted to one spot, have been given a place of honour in all ancient religious traditions. Some trees live more than a thousand years, but even the most short-lived, such as the fast-growing poplars and alders, outlive many people who survive long enough to have children. Plant a tree in your garden, and you are probably providing wood, shade and beauty to the next generation. The world will change around it, but the tree, one hopes, will remain. Along country roads around here, there are places where the houses have disappeared, but gnarled apple trees and lilacs survive as evidence of habitation. In Japan, old ginkgo trees were believed to be the only members of the plant world capable of loyalty, and some were thought to have died for their masters.

Trees have a presence that is both strong and peaceful. They survive hardship and so become symbolic of steadfastness and bravery. They offer all of the four ancient elements: air, water, fire and earth.

There is no better way to find an oasis than to look for trees, and conversely, the appearance of trees on the horizon may be the first evidence of an island in the ocean. Where trees grow, we can live too. Trees can be used to make buildings and to heat them. They give fruit and flowers, sweet sap and medicinal bark. They are homes for many animals and birds, and they shelter human homes from both summer heat and winter winds. According to recent research by the United States Department of Agriculture (USDA) Forest Service, trees in the landscape can save homeowners 5 to 15 percent of their annual heating cost and as much as half of their annual cooling cost.

What wondrous life is this I lead!
Ripe apples drop about my head;
The luscious clusters of the vine
Upon my mouth do crush their wine;
The nectarine and curious peach
Into my hands themselves do reach;
Stumbling on melons as I pass,
Insnared with flowers, I fall on grass.
—Andrew Marvell, "The Garden," 1681

The sacred tree—which shows up in the story of the Garden of Eden in two forms, the Tree of Knowledge, which is the bearer of forbidden fruit, and the Tree of Life, which grants immortality—has found a counterpart in myth and legend worldwide. In the Celtic past, every tribe had a sacred tree at the centre of its territory, embodying the security and integrity of that group. As this tree was considered a tree of life, invaders who felled it could demoralize and weaken their enemies.

"Once upon a time," wrote Pliny the Elder during the first century A.D., "trees were the temples of the deities, and in conformity with primitive ritual, simple country places even now dedicate a tree of exceptional height to a god; nor do we pay greater worship to images shining with gold and ivory than to the forests and to the very silences that they contain."

Sacred groves around the world are places of prayer and magic. In Africa, according to Dominique Zahan, sacred groves may consist of the tangled branches of thorn trees (acacia) around a central clearing, which is used for initiations and is barred to outsiders. "But if the grove, sacred in its entirety, constitutes the image of knowledge, then the interior clearing represents the end of the path toward learning; the sky, the abode of pure souls, the 'holy' space par excellence." This is the image—celebrated over and over in song and story and in art such as that of Emily Carr—of a space in the forest surrounded by tall trees, hushed by a screen of vegetation that also bars the intrusions of the outside world. The light shimmers through the foliage into a central clearing: nature as cathedral.

151

To what extent is one's garden, even with just one or two trees, a sacred grove? Trees in gardens always become centres of attention. They are too big and long-lived to ignore. Children climb them and swing from them. The trees near or around the houses of our childhood become part of our life stories. Even a small garden can have its tree—a small tree, of course. A tree that fits the garden makes sense beyond the fact that if it is too big, it will crowd out the rest of the garden and may be a hazard in a windstorm or a menace to overhead wires. Another drawback of a too large tree is that it offers only trunk. In a small space, one wants branches or foliage that begin around knee level and a top that is not much higher than eye level—a people tree rather than a forest tree. A tree does not have to be huge to lend a garden an aura of sacredness, but the older the tree is, the better it does the job.

And on the banks, on both sides of the river, there will grow all kinds of trees for food. Their leaves will not wither nor their fruit fail, but they will bear fresh fruit every month, because the water for them flows from the sanctuary. Their fruit will be for food, and their leaves for healing.
—Ezekiel 47:12

The garden has always been a place where people and plants interact, with transformation on both sides. Every plant in the garden has a story, and that story is as much human as botanical. A garden is, in a sense, a unique combination of stories brought together in a particular plot, be it a balcony or a farmyard. The botanical part of the story includes, among other things, the plant's place of origin, its eventual size and probable life span, its method of pollination and its preferred soil and temperature range.

It includes, too, the plant's companion pests and partners: fuchsia brings hummingbirds, milkweed brings monarch butterflies, borage brings bees. On the other hand, cabbage brings cabbage worms, potato brings Colorado potato beetles, cucumber brings cucumber beetles. The odd truth about these last three pests is that all are attracted to plant substances which are poisonous or bad-tasting to most creatures: mustard oil in cabbage, solanine in potatoes, cucurbitacins in cucumbers. Grow a "burpless" cucumber with less of the bitter cucurbitacins, and you will have fewer cucumber beetles. Obviously, people are not the only creatures interacting with plants. Every plant has its retinue, like a prince with his servants and his enemies. When we bring in the plant, we bring in everything else along with it.

The human aspect of the story is one of transplanting or sowing, often of selection and hybridization and of use for food, textiles, fuel, building materials, decoration or medicine. As soon as a plant is brought into a garden—and sometimes long before that—the human aspect becomes part of its story. As much as gardeners might love the idea of growing wild-flowers, we cannot really help do-mesticating them. Once they are in-side our boundaries, the transfor-mation has begun. Take a California poppy to North Dakota, and the seeds that make it through the very un-Californian winter will be better adapted to the North Dakota climate than the ones that did not survive.

We can in fact only define a weed, mutatis mutandis, in terms of the well-known definition of dirt—as matter out of place. What we call a weed is in fact merely a plant growing where we do not want it.
—E.J. Salisbury, The Living Garden, 1935

Next spring's seedlings represent a domesticated strain in the making. Even a California poppy grown in a California garden will, over generations, adapt to that microclimate. If the seeds were purchased or taken from plants whose ancestor's seeds were purchased, they represent the outcome of human selection, perhaps for a certain colour or size. Nothing alive is static. Plants may not be able to walk, but they are changing all the time, as are we.

Many other garden plants have histories that can, and do, fill volumes. Some have stories so intertwined with those of humanity that we have shaped them into what they are, just as surely as if they were pieces of sculpture. Preferred seeds and preferred plants have been selected, perhaps purposely crossbred, for so long that the original model is now hidden deep in the plant's genetic matter. A couple of extreme examples are head lettuce and corn, common vegetables that have no direct ancestors in nature. Head lettuce began as a Mediterranean herb, corn as a South American grass. Now, one is a huge globe of delicious leaves, and the other a huge head of seeds.

There are many more of these living sculptures in the garden, and countless numbers have been turned out in this century because of speedy methods of hybridization and mutation. Treat a plant with radiation or botanical hormones, and something more popular than the parent may grow. Genetic matter may be moved from species to species. When species are crossed, hybrids result, often bigger, brighter and more productive than their parents.

The human stories that garden plants tell are largely stories of human preference and the whims of fashion. Why choose a particular plant, after all? Until a couple of centuries ago, plants grew in gardens because they were edible or medicinal. Ornamentation was a secondary virtue, although many useful plants, from roses to sunflowers, offered both ornamental and edible benefits. The most venerable and useful of the plants are accompanied by their own myths and legends. Their botanical names may hint at their stories. A few examples among the A's are achillea (yarrow), named for Achilles, the Greek god who used the plant for healing; artemisia (southernwood, wormwood, tarragon), for Artemis, moon goddess of fertility; asclepias (milkweed), for Asklepios, the Greek god of medicine; atropa (deadly nightshade), for Atropes, one of three Greek goddesses who lived at the foot of the tree of life, cutting the thread of mortality.

I do not scorn weeds. As a matter of fact, there are some instances where they are necessary for the garden. The question of propriety is decided by the dialogue between man and weed.
—Shimpei Kusano, poet and gardener

Some of these plants, such as nightshade, are mood-altering or hallucinogenic and so have been grown for reasons of ritual or magic. In small amounts, their active ingredients may be medicinal, in larger amounts, poisonous. Especially important in this regard are plants that contain alkaloids, physiologically active substances whose names end with the suffix "ine," such as nicotine (from the tobacco plant, *Nicotiana tabacum*), caffeine (from the coffee tree, *Coffea arabica*), morphine (from the opium poppy, *Papaver somniferum*), cocaine (*Erythroxylon coca*) and quinine (*Cinchona officinalis*) as well as the extremely poisonous strychnine (from *Strychnos nux-vomica*) and aconitine, from monkshood (*Aconitum napellus*). It may not matter to today's gardener that monkshood was once used as a poison on arrowheads or that *Artemisia absinthium* is the force behind absinthe, a dangerous *eau de vie* to which Toulouse Lautrec and his friends were fatally attracted, but it may matter very much that the former has beautiful blue flowers which resemble those of its cousin the delphinium and that the latter has pretty greyish leaves, tolerates dry soil and goes well with bright poppies. Choosing what to grow is now largely a matter of aesthetics.

But our own aesthetic preferences are bounded by what is available. Why do gardeners grow pretty much the same plants, given a few slight variations in colour and size? Climate does narrow the possibilities, of course. Still, of the thousands and thousands of plant species on earth, gardeners concentrate upon just a few hundred, and a select few of these are grown by almost everybody: lawn grasses, tomatoes, tulips. The plants we choose have, by and large, proved to be good companions for us. They are not unruly, pushy, unpredictable, difficult or unpleasant.

Besides, howevermuch the plants in our own gardens resemble those in other people's gardens, ours have unique stories. This is their final chapter, still being written. Some of our plants come from nurseries, and we know when, where and why we purchased them, where we planted them and how they fared. Some we have grown with our own hands from seed or cutting. Some have come from neighbours or family. Seeds may have been passed down through genera-

On the first of May, with my comrades of the catechism class, I laid lilac, camomile and roses before the altar of the Virgin, and returned full of pride to show my "blessed posy." My mother laughed her irreverent laugh and, looking at my bunch of flowers, which was bringing the may-bug into the sitting-room right under the lamp, she said: "D'you suppose it wasn't already blessed before?"
—*Colette,* Sido, 1922

tions and cuttings handed over already potted up. In 1735, Peter Collinson of London wrote to American John Custis: "I think there is no Greater pleasure than to be Communicative and oblige others....It not only preserves a Friendly Society but secures our Collections, for if one does not raise a seed perhaps another does & if one Looses a plant another can Supply him." It is upon such neighbourly exchange that the preservation of heirloom plant varieties depends.

As every gardener knows, however, not all plants grow in the garden by invitation. Some of the most faithful of our plant partners are the ones we call weeds. These species take advantage of fertilized, watered soil and the increased diet of sunlight that comes from felled forests and plowed fields. They accompany us wherever we go and take root wherever we break the soil. To the New World came a host of species now so common in North America that they seem to belong here: dandelions, thistles, lamb's quarters, burdock, mustard, nettles, mullein, oxeye daisies, chicory, pigweed, purslane, ground ivy and almost everything else which colonizes roadsides where they were unknown a couple of centuries ago. All of these, incidentally, have nutritional and medicinal qualities for which they have been valued in the past. But now we perceive them only as too eager to dog our steps. Weeds crash our parties, making demands upon our already limited resources of time and space. They want to play ragtime tunes on a xylophone while we are trying to create hushed string quartets in the perennial borders and Sousa marches in the rows of carrots and corn. They are our companions, but we love them about as much as we do the fleas on our dogs and cats.

Science, or para-science, tells us that geraniums bloom better if they are spoken to. But a kind word every now and then is really quite enough. Too much attention, like too much feeding and weeding and hoeing, inhibits and embarrasses them.
—*Victoria Glendinning*, Green Words, *1986*

We are choosy about what grows in our gardens. Weeds thrive, and we poison them or pull them out, selecting instead more difficult things that must be watered, pruned, deadheaded and then protected in winter. Plant nurseries and seed companies thrive because we gardeners do not want what grows naturally, and furthermore, we fill our gardens not once but over and over.

Most of what we buy dies. Vegetables and flowering annuals meant for a short, productive life in the heat of summer die, but much more of what dies is supposedly longer-lived. Gardeners are forever testing the limits of plant adaptation, intentionally or not, and putting species adapted to warmth into cold places or things adapted to shade into sunny places or things that like rocky ground into wet humus. Even if they are put in the right places, newly planted things left to their own devices, unweeded and unwatered by gardening novices, will probably die.

In the nursery, they thrived and would likely have continued to do so if they could have stayed put. The fact is that plants are just not meant to move about, any more than we are meant to stay rooted. But garden plants must bend to our will and must be lifted, carted, uprooted and transplanted wherever we go. Plants newly arrived in our gardens are very vulnerable. Nothing in millions of years of evolution prepared them for this. So they must be shaded and deeply watered and fussed over until they can make it on their own, more or less.

It would be a great help if a plant could point to the spot where it would like to be or could just get up and walk to that other flower border a few feet away. Then, of course, my entire garden might march next door, where it could be cared for by somebody else. Fortunately for us, plants have no choice but to be endlessly patient with us. They cannot run away when we decide to prune them to look like topknots. They cannot call out when we forget to water them. They cannot hide when we decide to dig them up and cart them to the other side of the path.

And this is why we love them, and love our gardens. Whenever we want to continue our long exploration of what it means to be alive with all the elements that are part of the garden, everything is there, waiting for us. And we are part of the garden too.

Plant Choice

Choosing what plants to grow in my gardens has depended, at the outset, upon what was already there. Sometimes I have liked what the previous gardener has chosen, sometimes not. There have always been native trees too. Then, my own taste, patience, ability and budget has had a bearing, along with what is available from nurseries and seed companies or what other gardeners offer.

All of this is limited by climate and the peculiarities of the garden. One fortunate thing about the garden is that choices are not irreversible. Anything can be changed, and within reason, almost any plant can be moved. The larger the plant, the more carefully this must be done. But there are certain things I have learned to be wary of at the outset.

Some plants are so invasive that the gardener may spend months, years or a lifetime pulling them out once they have a toehold. I have struggled, at various times, with lily-of-the-valley, Chinese lantern, yarrow, common lilac, horseradish, tansy and mint, none of which are classified as weeds. Here are a few more things to think about at least twice before planting, because all have spreading runners or roots: goutweed, snow-in-summer, ribbon grass, sumac, Mexican bamboo and almost any other member of the genus *Polygonum*. If you want these perennials—and all of them have qualities to recommend them—it is not a bad idea to put them in their own beds, like children with measles, so that you can mow around them. Or they can go in containers so that they cannot spread. Some gardeners bury containers with just the rim showing so that the plant appears to be part of the ground-level landscape. Just remember that any container, even a buried one, needs more care in watering than the surrounding garden. Annual or biennial plants that spread profusely by seed, such as chamomile, violets, forget-me-nots and datura are easy to control. As soon as the seedlings appear, scrape the ground with a hoe or, if the area is small, a trowel.

Another group I am wary of are the marginally hardy—or downright tender—perennials. An investment of a few dollars for a herbaceous perennial known to be chancy may pay off by, at the least, giving colour for a year or, at best, turning out to be a long-term success, but trees that die after the first winter can mean the loss of a disheartening amount of money and time. I once lost several new fruit trees because they were simply too tender to survive winter in my garden. Local nurseries that sell these plants may be inspired by optimism, ignorance or dishonesty. Ironically, these are often the most expensive things they sell. If I have never seen a particular species growing locally, I am cautious. For the backbone of the landscape, I depend on plants known for hardiness in my area and grow more tender things just for the adventure of it.

May /June 95

Bibliography

General

Ackerman, Diane, *A Natural History of the Senses*, Random House, New York, 1990.

Bonnefoy, Yves, ed., *Mythologies*, vol. 2, University of Chicago Press, Chicago, 1991.

Capon, Brian, *Botany for Gardeners: An Introduction and Guide*, Timber Press, Portland, Oregon, 1990.

Evans, Ivor, ed., *Brewer's Dictionary of Phrase and Fable*, Harper & Row, New York, 1981.

Fogg, C.E., *The Growth of Plants*, Penguin, Harmondsworth, 1963.

Gibbons, Bob, *The Secret Life of Flowers: A Guide to Plant Biology*, Blandford, London, 1990.

Graves, Robert, *The Greek Myths*, vol. 1, Penguin, Harmondsworth, 1955.

Holm, Eigil, *The Biology of Flowers*, Penguin, Harmondsworth, 1979.

Hunt, Peter, ed., *The Garden Lover's Com-panion*, Eyre Methuen, London, 1974.

Jones, Hamlyn G., *Plants and Microclimate*, second ed., Cambridge University Press, Cambridge, 1992.

Langenheim, J.H. and K.V. Thimann, *Botany: Plant Biology and Its Relation to Human Affairs*, Wiley, New York, 1982.

Lurker, Manfred, *The Gods and Symbols of Ancient Egypt*, Thames & Hudson, London, 1974.

Meense, Bastian and Sean Morris, *The Sex Life of Flowers*, Facts on File, New York, 1984.

New Larousse Encyclopedia of Mythology, second ed., Prometheus Press, London, 1972.

Onians, R.B., *The Origins of European Thought: About the Body, the Mind, the Soul, the World, Time and Fate*, Cambridge University Press, Cambridge, 1951.

Percival, Mary, *Floral Biology*, Pergamon Press, Oxford, 1965.

Plinius Secundus (Pliny the Elder), *Nat-*

ural History, Book 12, Harvard University Press, Cambridge, Massachusetts, 1966.

Raven, Peter, Ray F. Evert and Helena Curtis, *Biology of Plants*, second ed., Worth, New York, 1976.

On Gardens

Dash, Robert, "The Changing of the Garden," *House and Garden*, February 1986, p. 30.

Epton, Nina, *Josephine and Her Children*, Weidenfeld & Nicolson, London, 1975.

Lawrence, Elizabeth, *Gardening for Love: The Market Bulletins*, Duke University Press, Durham, North Carolina, 1987.

Osler, Mirabel, *A Gentle Plea for Chaos: The Enchantment of Gardening*, Simon & Schuster, New York, 1989.

Peitgen, H.O. and P.H. Richter, *The Beauty of Fractals*, Springer-Verlag, Berlin, 1986.

On Light

Aimers High Quality Bulbs, Aurora, Ontario, Autumn 1993, p. 28.

Beston, Henry, *Herbs and the Earth*, David R. Godine, Boston, 1990 (orig. pub. by Henry Beston, 1935).

Clevenger, Sarah, "Flower Pigments, *Scientific American*, vol. 212, 1964, pp. 85-92.

Elliott, G.F. Scott, *The Wonders of the Plant World*, Seeley & Co., London, 1910.

"Flower Color Influences Garden Mood," *Today's Garden*, National Garden Bureau, Downers Grove, Illinois, May 1993.

Frank, Silvia, "Carotenoids," *Scientific American*, vol. 195, 1956, pp. 80-86.

McElroy, William D. and Bentley Glass, eds., *A Symposium on Light and Life*, The Johns Hopkins Press, Baltimore, 1961.

Pennisi, Elizabeth, "True Blue: Molecules Stack Up to Color Flowers," *Science News*, vol. 42, November 21, 1991, p. 186.

Perényi, Eleanor, *Green Thoughts: A Writer in the Garden*, Vintage, New York, 1981.

Robberecht, Robert, "Environmental Photobiology," *The Science of Photobiology*, second ed., Plenum, New York, 1989.

Sackville-West, Vita, *The Illustrated Garden Book*, Michael Joseph, London, 1986.

Sackville-West, Vita, *A Joy of Gardening*, Harper & Row, New York, 1958.

Seliger, H.H. and W.D. McElroy, *Light: Physical and Biological Action*, Academic Press, New York, 1965.

Stokes, Donald W., *A Guide to Nature in Winter*, Little, Brown & Co., Boston, 1976.

White, Katharine S., *Onward and Upward in the Garden*, Farrar, Straus, Giroux, New York, 1958.

Wilder, Louise Beebe, *Color in My Garden*, Atlantic Monthly Press, New York, 1990 (orig. pub. as *Colour in My Garden*, 1918).

On Air

Amthor, Jeffrey S., *Respiration and Crop Productivity*, Springer-Verlag, New York, 1989.

Baldwin, C.S., *Windbreaks on the Farm*, publication 527, Ontario Ministry of Agriculture and Food, Toronto, 1984.

Bennett, Jennifer, *Lilies of the Hearth: The Historical Relationship Between Women and Plants*, Camden House, Camden East, Ontario, 1991.

Darnton, John, "Bulgaria's Rare Rose Oil for Perfumes may be Rarer after a Bad Winter," *The New York Times*, June 26, 1980, p. 10.

Devereux, Paul, *Earthmind,* Harper & Row, New York, 1989.

Hampton, F.A., *The Scent of Flowers and Leaves: Its Purpose in Relation to Man*, Dulan & Co., London, 1925.

Harp, H.F. and W.A. Cumming, *Hedges for the Prairies*, publication 1153, Agriculture Canada, Ottawa, 1974.

Hawkins, Henry, *Parthenia Sacra*, John Cousturier, London, 1633.

"How Air Pollution Affects Vegetation," *Facts About Phytotoxicology*, Ontario Ministry of the Environment, Summer 1983, p. 3.

Luria, S.E., *Life, the Unfinished Experiment*, Scribner's, New York, 1973.

Mulcahy, David L., "Bios: Rise of the Angiosperms," *Natural History*, vol. 90, no. 9, September 1983, pp. 30-35.

Nash, J. Madeleine, "How Did Life Begin," *Time*, vol. 142, no. 15, October 11, 1993, pp. 45-48.

Osler, Mirabel, *A Gentle Plea for Chaos: The Enchantment of Gardening*, Simon & Schuster, New York, 1989.

Page, Russell, *The Education of a Gardener*, William Collins Sons & Co. Ltd., London, 1962.

Parkinson, John, *Paradisi in sole, paradisus terrestris*, Methuen, London, 1904 (orig. pub. London, 1629).

Pedgley, David, *Windborne Pests and Diseases: Meteorology of Airborne Organisms*, John Wiley & Sons, New York, 1982.

Prescod, Alfred W., "Growing Indoor Plants as Air Purifiers," *Pappus*, vol. 9, no. 4, Autumn 1990, pp. 13-20.

Rohde, Eleanour Sinclair, *The Scented Garden*, The Medici Society Ltd., London, 1931.

Stone, Doris, "Biological Aspects of Scent," *Gardening for Fragrance*, handbook 121, vol. 45, no. 3, Brooklyn Botanic Garden, New York, 1989.

Thomas, Lewis, *The Lives of a Cell: Notes of a Biology Watcher*, Bantam, Toronto, 1975.

Tyndall, John, *Essays on the Floating-Matter of the Air*, D. Appleton & Co., New York, 1882.

Van Horn, G.A., "Fungi Outnumber Pollen, State Allergists Learn," Pennsylvania State University, University Park, Pennsylvania, 1979.

Weintraub, Pamela, "Scentimental Journeys," *Omni*, April 1986, pp. 52, 114-116.

Williams, G. and P. Williams, eds., "Essential Oils vs. Bean Weevils," *HortIdeas*, vol. 10, no. 8, August 1983, p. 92.

Wolverton, W.L., *A Study of Interior Landscape Plants for Indoor Air Pollution Abatement: An Interim Report*, NASA, October 1988.

Zimmer, Heinrich, *Myths and Symbols in Indian Art and Civilization*, Bollinger, Princeton, New Jersey, 1946.

On Warmth

Andrews, C.J., "Low-Temperature Stress in Field and Forage Crop Production —An Overview," *Canadian Journal of Plant Science*, vol. 67, October 1987, pp. 1121-1133.

Chandler, W.H., "Cold Resistance in Horticultural Plants," *Proceedings of the American Society of Horticultural Science*, vol. 64, 1954, pp. 552-572.

Cook, Robert E., "The Cold Facts of Winter Wheat," *Natural History*, vol. 92, no. 1, January 1983, p. 24.

Culpeper, Nicholas, *Culpeper's Complete Herbal*, W. Foulsham & Co., New York (reprinted from *The English Physician* and *The English Physician Enlarged*, 1652, 1653).

Ehrlich, Paul R., *The Machinery of Nature: The Living World Around Us and How It Works*, Simon & Schuster, New York, 1986.

Falk, Dean, "A Good Brain is Hard to Cool," *Natural History*, vol. 102, no. 8, August 1993, p. 65.

Fitzpatrick, E.A., *An Introduction to Soil Science*, Oliver & Boyd, Edinburgh, 1974.

Heschong, Lisa, "Thermal Necessity," *Natural History*, vol. 90, no. 10, October 1981, p. 32.

Jones, Hamlyn G., *Plants and Microclimate*, second ed., Cambridge University Press, Cambridge, 1992.

Knutson, Roger, "Flowers that Make Heat While the Sun Shines," *Natural History*, vol. 90, no. 10, October 1981.

Longley, Richmond W., "The Frost-Free Period in Alberta," *Canadian Journal of Plant Science*, vol. 47, May 1967, p. 249.

Marchand, Peter J., *Life in the Cold: An Introduction to Winter Ecology*, University Press of New England, Hanover, New Hampshire, 1987.

Ouellet, C.E. and L.C. Sherk, "Woody Ornamental Plant Zonation," *Canadian Journal of Plant Science*, vol. 47, 1967, pp. 231, 339, 351.

Parkinson, John, *Paradisi in sole, paradisus terrestris*, Methuen, London, 1904 (orig. pub. London, 1629).

Pedgley, David, *Windborne Pests and Diseases: Meteorology of Airborne Organisms*, John Wiley & Sons, New York, 1982.

Quamme, H.A., "Low-Temperature Stress in Canadian Horticultural Crops—An Overview," *Canadian Journal of Plant Science*, vol. 67, October 1987, pp. 1135-1149.

Robinson, Michael D., "Death and Dancing on the Sun-Baked Dunes of Namibia," *Natural History*, vol. 102, no. 8, August 1993, p. 28.

Scott, Ray G., *How to Build Your Own Underground Home*, second ed., Tab, Blue Ridge, Pennsylvania, 1972.

Stokes, Donald W., *A Guide to Nature in Winter*, Little, Brown & Co., Boston, 1976.

Teskey, B.J.E., "Critical Temperatures for Fruit Blossoms," Agdex 210, Ontario Ministry of Agriculture and Food, July 1972.

Villiers, Trevor A., *Dormancy and the Survival of Plants*, Edward Arnold, London, 1975.

Weiser, C.J., "Cold Resistance and Injury in Woody Plants," *Science*, vol. 169, 1970, pp. 1269-1278.

Williams, G. and P. Williams, eds., "Root Hardiness of Selected Woody Ornamentals," *HortIdeas*, vol. 2, no. 12, December 1985.

On Earth

Bates, T.E., "Chemical and Organic Fertilizers," Agdex 540, Ontario Ministry of Agriculture and Food, September 1978.

Bates, T.E. and T.H. Lane, "Soil Acidity and Liming," Agdex 534, Ontario Ministry of Agriculture and Food, November 1979.

Beston, Henry, *Herbs and the Earth*, David R. Godine, Boston, 1990 (orig. pub. by Henry Beston, 1935).

Bridges, E.M., *World Soils*, Cambridge University Press, Cambridge, 1970.

Darwin, Charles, *The Formation of Vegetable Mould Through the Action of Worms*, John Murray, London, 1881.

Edwards, C.A. and J.R. Lofty, *Biology of Earthworms*, Chapman & Hall, London, 1972.

Fitzpatrick, E.A., *An Introduction to Soil Science*, Oliver & Boyd, Edinburgh, 1974.

Kramer, Paul J., *Water Relations of Plants*, Academic Press, New York, 1983.

Laverack, M.S., *The Physiology of Earthworms*, Pergamon Press, New York, 1963.

Olsen, R.A., R.B. Clark and J.H. Bennett, "The Enhancement of Soil Fertility by Plant Roots," *American Scientist*, vol. 69, July-August 1981, pp. 378-384.

Organic Matter: The Life of the Soil, bulletin 459, Ontario Agricultural College, Toronto, 1952.

Parkinson, John, *Paradisi in sole, paradisus terrestris*, Methuen, London, 1904 (orig. pub. London, 1629).

Poincelot, Raymond P., *The Biochemistry and Methodology of Composting*, bulletin 754, The Connecticut Agricultural Experiment Station, New Haven, Connecticut, September 1975.

Russell, Sir Edward John, *The World of the Soil*, Collins, London, 1957.

"Soils," *Plants & Gardens: Brooklyn Botanic Garden Record*, vol. 42, no. 2, 1986.

Tilth: Soil Supplement, vol. 8, no. 1 & 2, Arlington, Washington, 1982.

Wright, Richardson, *The Practical Book of Outdoor Flowers*, Garden City, New York, 1924.

On Stone

Beazley, Mitchell, *Simple Life Forms*, Mitchell Beazley Encyclopaedias Ltd., London, 1980.

Burland, Nicholson, Osborne, *Mythologies of the Americas*, Hamlyn, London, 1970.

Elliott, G.F. Scott, *The Wonders of the Plant World*, Seeley & Co., London, 1910.

Faul, H. and C. Faul, *It Began With a Stone*, John Wiley & Sons, New York, 1983.

Ferguson, Katharine, ed., *Rock Gardens: A Harrowsmith Gardener's Guide*, Camden House, Camden East, Ontario, 1988.

Gauri, K.L. and J.A. Gwinn, eds., *Fourth International Congress on the Deterioration and Preservation of Stone Objects*, University of Louisville, Louisville, Kentucky, 1982.

Gordon, J.E., *The New Science of Strong Materials: Or Why You Don't Fall Through the Floor*, second ed., Penguin, London, 1976.

Hearn, Lafcadio, "My Garden in Tokyo," in *The Garden Lover's Companion*, ed. Peter Hunt, Eyre Methuen, London, 1974.

"Japanese Gardens," *Quatre-Temps*, Montreal Botanical Garden, vol. 12, no. 2, Spring 1988.

Lockyer, Norman, *The Meteorite Hypothesis*, Macmillan & Co., London, 1890.

Ohashi, Haruzo, *The Japanese Garden*, Graphic-sha, Tokyo, 1986.

Prest, John, *The Garden of Eden: The Botanic Garden and the Re-Creation of Paradise*, Yale University Press, New Haven, Connecticut, 1981.

Sackville-West, Vita, *A Joy of Gardening*, Harper & Row, New York, 1958.

Shackley, Myra, *Rocks and Man*, George Allen & Unwin, Boston, 1977.

Simkiss, Kenneth and Karl Wilbur, *Biomineralization: Cell Biology and Mineral Deposition*, Academic Press, San Diego, 1989.

Winkler, E.M., *Stone: Properties, Durability in Man's Environment*, second ed., Springer-Verlag, New York, 1975.

Yoshikawa, Isao, *Japanese Stone Gardens*, Graphic-sha, Tokyo, 1992.

On Water

Chadwick, Douglas H., "Rocky Shores," in *The Curious Naturalist,* National Geographic Society, Washington, D.C., 1991.

Coder, Kim D., "Using Gray Water," *Grounds Maintenance*, vol. 26, no. 3., March 1991, pp. 16, 20, 22, 25.

Dewar, Lindsay, *The Holy Spirit and Modern Thought*, Harper & Bros., New York, 1959.

Dundes, Alan, ed., *The Flood Myth*, University of California Press, Berkeley, 1988.

Fenner, Michael, *Seed Ecology*, Chapman & Hall, London, 1985.

Kramer, Paul J., *Water Relations of Plants*, Academic Press, New York, 1983.

La Motte-Fouque, Friedrich, *Undine and Other Stories*, trans. Sir Edmund Gosse, Oxford University Press, London, 1932.

Nakajima, Ken, "The Japanese Garden of the Montreal Botanical Garden," *Quatre-Temps*, Montreal Botanical Garden, vol. 12, no. 2, Spring 1988, p. 16.

Neilsen, Jackson, Cary, Evans, eds., *Soil Water*, American Society of Agronomy and Soil Science Society of America, Madison, Wisconsin, 1972.

Parrinder, G., ed., *World Religions*, Facts on File, New York, 1971.

Piggott, Julie, *Japanese Mythology*, Paul Hamlyn, London, 1969.

165

Toolson, Eric, "In the Sonoran Desert, Cicadas Court, Mate and Waste Water," *Natural History,* vol. 102, no. 8, August 1993, p. 38.

Vogel, Steven, *Life's Devices,* Princeton University Press, Princeton, New Jersey, 1988.

Wilder, Louise Beebe, *Color in My Garden,* Atlantic Monthly Press, New York, 1990 (orig. published as *Colour in My Garden,* 1918).

Williams, G. and P. Williams, eds., "Fluoridated Water Can Harm Plants," *Hort-Ideas,* vol. 2, no. 6, June 1985.

Xeriscape: A Guide to Developing a Water-Wise Landscape, Cooperative Extension Service, The University of Georgia, Athens, Georgia, 1992.

On Paths

Astrov, Margot, ed., *The Winged Serpent: American Indian Prose and Poetry,* Beacon Press, Boston, 1992.

Huxley, Anthony, *An Illustrated History of Gardening,* Paddington, New York, 1978.

"Japanese Gardens," *Quatre-Temps,* Montreal Botanical Garden, vol. 12, no. 2, Spring 1988.

Lurker, Manfred, *The Gods and Symbols of Ancient Egypt,* Thames & Hudson, London, 1974.

Ohashi, Haruzo, *The Japanese Garden,* Graphic-sha, Tokyo, 1986.

Peitgen, H.O. and P.H. Richter, *The Beauty of Fractals,* Springer-Verlag, Berlin, 1986.

Perényi, Eleanor, *Green Thoughts: A Writer in the Garden,* Vintage, New York, 1981.

Prest, John, *The Garden of Eden: The Botanic Garden and the Re-Creation of Paradise,* Yale University Press, New Haven, Connecticut, 1981.

Puhvel, Martin, *The Crossroads in Folklore and Myth,* Peter Lang, New York, 1989.

Taylor, Patrick, *The Garden Path,* Simon & Schuster, New York, 1991.

Trombold, Charles D., ed., *Ancient Road Networks and Settlement Hierarchies in the New World,* Cambridge University Press, Cambridge, 1991.

Zahan, Dominique, *The Religion, Spirituality and Thought of Traditional Africa,* University of Chicago Press, Chicago, 1970.

On Walls

Bailey, L.H., "The Spirit of the Home Garden," in *How to Make a Flower Garden,* Doubleday, New York, 1910.

Burnett, Frances Hodgson, *The Secret Garden,* J.B. Lippincott, Philadelphia, 1962.

Carter, G.A. and A.H. Teramura, "Vine Photosynthesis and Relationships to Climbing Mechanics in a Forest Understory," *American Journal of Botany,* vol. 75, no. 7, 1988, pp. 1011-1018.

"Chinese Gardens," *Quatre-Temps,* Montreal Botanical Garden, vol. 15, no. 2, Summer 1991.

Hedges for Canadian Gardens, Agriculture Canada, Ottawa, publication number 899, 1975.

Huxley, Anthony, *An Illustrated History of Gardening,* Paddington, New York, 1978.

Hyland, Bob, "Annual Vines for Terrace Gardeners," *The Green Scene,* January 1986, pp. 28-30.

Jekyll, Gertrude, *The Gardener's Essential Gertrude Jekyll,* Godine, Boston, 1986 (orig. pub. 1964).

Malmberg, Torsten, *Human Territoriality,* Mouton, The Hague, 1980.

Nice, Margaret Morse, "The Role of Territory in Bird Life," *The American Midland Naturalist,* vol. 26, 1941, p. 468.

Paterson, Allen, *Designing a Garden,* Camden House, Camden East, Ontario, 1992.

Sackville-West, Vita, *The Illustrated Garden Book,* Michael Joseph, London, 1986.

Symonds, Harry, *Fences,* McGraw-Hill Ryerson, Toronto, 1958.

Waldron, Arthur, *The Great Wall of China: From History to Myth*, Cambridge University Press, Cambridge, 1990.

Woody Climbers and Ground Covers, publication number 1017, Agriculture Canada, Ottawa, 1973.

On Sex

Abell, Annette, Erik Ernst and Jens Peter Bonde, "High Sperm Density Among Members of Organic Farmers' Association," *The Lancet*, vol. 343, no. 8911, June 11, 1994, p. 1498.

Barber, Lynn, *The Heyday of Natural History, 1820-1870*, Jonathan Cape, London, 1980.

Brown, Emerson Jr., "Hortus Inconclusus: The Significance of Priapus and Pyramus and Thisbe in the Merchant's Tale," *The Chaucer Review*, vol. 4, no. 1, 1970, pp. 31-34.

Carlsen, E., A. Giwercman et al., "Evidence for Decreasing Quality of Semen During Past 50 Years," *British Medical Journal*, vol. 305, no. 6854, 1992, pp. 609-613.

Chaucer, Geoffrey, *The Parlement of Foulys*, ed. D.S. Brewer, Thomas Nelson & Sons Ltd., London, 1960.

Comito, Terry, *The Idea of the Garden in the Renaissance*, Rutgers University Press, New Brunswick, New Jersey, 1978.

Fairclough, H.R., *Love of Nature Among the Greeks and Romans*, Longmans, Green & Co., New York, 1930.

Forsyth, Adrian, *A Natural History of Sex*, Chapters Publishing, Shelburne, Vermont, 1993.

Frazer, Sir James George, *The Golden Bough: A Study in Magic and Religion*, abridged ed., Macmillan, New York, 1958.

Gordon, Leslie, *Green Magic*, Viking, New York, 1977.

Grant, Michael and John Hazel, *Gods and Mortals in Classical Mythology*, Merriam-Webster, Springfield, Mississippi, 1973.

Grigson, Geoffrey, *The Goddess of Love: The Birth, Triumph, Death and Return of Aphrodite*, Constable, London, 1976.

Hale, Sarah Josepha, *Flora's Interpreter and Fortuna Flora*, Benjamin B. Mussey, Boston, 1850.

Hansband, Robert, ed., *The Complete Letters of Lady Mary Wortley Montagu*, vol. 1, Oxford University Press, London, 1965.

Harding, M. Esther, *Woman's Mysteries, Ancient and Modern*, G.P. Putnam's Sons, New York, 1971.

Heiser, Charles B. Jr., *Of Plants and People*, University of Oklahoma Press, Norman, Oklahoma, 1985.

Hill, Thomas, *The Gardener's Labyrinth*, ed. Richard Mabey, Oxford University Press, Oxford, 1987.

Hoffman, Richard L., *Ovid and the Canterbury Tales*, Oxford University Press, London, 1966.

James, E.O., *The Tree of Life*, E.J. Brill, Leiden, 1966.

Kramer, Samuel Noah, *The Sacred Marriage Rite: Aspects of Faith, Myth and Ritual in Ancient Sumer*, Indiana University Press, Bloomington, Indiana, 1969.

La Barre, Weston, *Muelos: A Stone Age Superstition About Sexuality*, Columbia University Press, New York, 1984.

Mea, Allan, *Darwin and His Flowers: The Key to Natural Selection*, Faber & Faber, London, 1977.

The Orphic Hymns, trans. Apostolos N. Athanassakis, Scholars Press, Missoula, Montana, 1977.

Paris, Ginette, *Pagan Meditations: The Worlds of Aphrodite, Artemis and Hestia*, trans. G. Moore, Spring Publications, Dallas, 1986.

Peattie, D.C., *An Almanac for Moderns*, G.P. Putnam's Sons, New York, 1935.

Pimentel, David and Lois Levitan, "Pesticides: Amounts Applied and Amounts Reaching Pests," *BioScience*, vol. 36, no. 2, 1986, pp. 86-91.

Pope, Rita Tragellas, "Bean Lore," in *Plant-Lore Studies*, The Folklore Society, London, 1984.

Stebbins, G.L., "The Flowering of Sex," *The Sciences*, May/June 1984, pp. 28-35.

Taberner, P.V., *Aphrodisiacs: The Science and the Myth*, Croom Helm, London, 1985.

Theocritus, *The Idylls*, trans. Robert Wells, Penguin, Harmondsworth, 1989.

The Travels of Marco Polo, Orion Press, New York, 1958.

Uemichi, Isao, "Japanese Plant-Lore: A Brief Survey," in *Plant-Lore Studies*, The Folklore Society, London, 1984.

Virgil, *Georgics*, Book Four, in *Virgil's Works*, trans. J.W. Mackail, The Modern Library, New York, 1934.

White Rose Nursery and Garden Guide, Unionville, Ontario, 1994.

On Plants

Bennett, Jennifer, *Lilies of the Hearth: The Historical Relationship Between Women and Plants*, Camden House, Camden East, Ontario, 1991.

Clark, A.J., "Flying Ointments," in Margaret Murray, *The Witch-Cult in Western Europe*, Oxford University Press, London, 1921.

Culpeper, Nicholas, *Culpeper's Complete Herbal*, W. Foulsham & Co., New York (reprinted from *The English Physician* and *The English Physician Enlarged*, 1652, 1653).

Lawrence, Elizabeth, *Gardening for Love: The Market Bulletins*, Duke University Press, Durham, North Carolina, 1987.

MacCana, Prionsias, *Celtic Mythology*, Hamlyn, London, 1920.

Stone, Doris, "The Armory—How Plants Protect Themselves," *Plants & Gardens: Brooklyn Botanic Garden Record*, vol. 40, no. 2, 1984, pp. 38-43.

Stuart, Malcolm, ed., *The Encyclopedia of Herbs and Herbalism*, Orbis, London, 1979.

White, Katharine S., *Onward and Upward in the Garden*, Farrar, Straus, Giroux, New York, 1958.

Williams, G. and P. Williams, eds., "City Dwellers: Plant Trees to Save Energy ...and Money!" *HortIdeas*, vol. 10, no. 12, December 1993.

Zahan, Dominique, *The Religion, Spirituality and Thought of Traditional Africa*, University of Chicago Press, Chicago, 1970.

Index

Permissions

I am grateful to the following authors, publishers and copyright owners for permission to excerpt quotations from their work.

Wendell Berry, *The Unsettling of America*, Sierra Club Books, San Francisco, 1977.

Henry Beston, *Herbs and the Earth,* David R. Godine Publisher, Inc., Boston, 1990 (originally published by Henry Beston, 1935).

Helen Chesnut, column in *The Vancouver Province*, October 1992.

Colette, *Sido*, 1922. Reprinted by permission of Martin Secker & Warburg, London, and Farrar, Straus & Giroux Inc., New York.

Colette, *Pour un herbier* (trans. Roger Stenhouse), 1949. Reprinted by permission of Weidenfeld and Nicolson Publishers, London.

Jeff Cox, "Paths of Least Resistance," *Harrowsmith Country Life*, vol. 8, no. 47, September/October 1993.

W.H. Davies, *My Garden,* Henry Holt and Company, Inc., New York, 1933.

Annie Dillard, *Pilgrim at Tinker Creek*, Harper & Row Publishers, New York, 1974. Copyright 1974 by Annie Dillard. Excerpt reprinted by permission of HarperCollins Publishers, Inc.

Timothy Findley, "From Stone Orchard: Wildwood," *Harrowsmith* magazine, vol. 18, no. 12, December 1993. Reprinted courtesy of Pebbles Productions, Cannington, Ontario.

Adrian Forsyth, *A Natural History of Sex*, Chapters Publishing, Shelburne, Vermont, 1993.

Robert Frost, "Mending Wall" in *The Poetry of Robert Frost*, edited by Edward Connery Lathem. Copyright 1967 by Lesley Frost Ballantine. Copyright 1928, 1930, 1939, 1969 by Henry Holt and Company, Inc. Reprinted with permission of Henry Holt and Company, New York.

Victoria Glendinning, *Green Words: The Sunday Times Book of Garden Quotations*, Quartet Books Ltd., London, 1986.

John Jerome, *Stone Work*, Viking Press. Copyright 1989 by John Jerome. Used by permission of Viking Penguin, a division of Penguin Books USA Inc.

Allen Lacy, *Allen Lacy's homeground*, Winter 1993, Linwood, New Jersey.

Yva Momatiuk and John Eastcott, for quotations by Betty Schlichting and Albert (Stonewall) Johnson from *In a Sea of Wind*, Camden House Publishing, Camden East, Ontario. Copyright 1991 by Yva Momatiuk and John Eastcott.

Mirabel Osler, *A Gentle Plea for Chaos: The Enchantment of Gardening*. Copyright 1989 by Mirabel Osler. Reprinted by permission of Simon & Schuster, Inc., New York.

Russell Page, *The Education of a Gardener*, William Collins & Co. Ltd., London, 1962.

Ginette Paris, *Pagan Meditations: The Worlds of Aphrodite, Artemis and Hestia*, trans. G. Moore, 1986. Reprinted courtesy of Mary Helen Sullivan, Spring Publications, Dallas.

Michael Pollan, *Second Nature*, 1991. Copyright 1991 by Michael Pollan. Reprinted by permission of Grove/Atlantic, Inc., New York.

G. Ragni and G McDermott, the song "Air," EMI Music Publishing Canada Ltd., Toronto.

Sir Edward John Russell, *The World of Soil*, Collins, London, 1957.

Vita Sackville-West, *In Your Garden Again*, Michael Joseph Ltd., London, 1953.

Reprinted courtesy of the Hon. Nigel Nicolson, executor of the estate of Vita Sackville-West.

Paul Simon, the song, "I Am a Rock." Copyright 1965/Copyright renewed Paul Simon.

Elizabeth Smart, *Elizabeth's Garden*, Coach House Press, 1989. Reprinted courtesy of Sebastian Bauker, literary executor to, and owner of, the Elizabeth Smart Literary Estate.

Hua Ling Chen Su, "Our Old Gardener," *Country Life Magazine*, February 16, 1951.

Rosemary Verey, *The Scented Garden*, Van Nostrand Reinhold, New York, 1981.

Steven Vogel, *Life's Devices*, Princeton University Press, Princeton, New Jersey, 1988.

Katharine S. White, *Onward and Upward in the Garden*, copyright 1979 by E.B. White. Reprinted by permission of Farrar, Straus & Giroux, Inc., New York.

Louise Beebe Wilder, *Color in My Garden*, Atlantic Monthly Press, New York, 1990 (originally published as *Colour in My Garden*, 1918). Copyright 1990 by Harrison Wilder Taylor. Reprinted by permission of Grove/Atlantic, Inc., New York.

While every effort has been made to trace the copyright holder and secure required reprint permission for quotations, in a few cases, this may not have been possible. I apologize for any oversights.